Petersfield

A PICTORIAL PAST

To the memory of
William Etherington,
Brickmaker and Farmer,
who knew Petersfield
and its countryside well.

Sean Street

**With the full text of The History of Petersfield by
Rev. J. Williams M.A., Curate of St. Peter's Church.**

Ensign
PUBLICATIONS

First published in 1989 by Ensign Publications.
© Sean Street, 1989.

Ensign Publications
A division of Hampshire Books Ltd.,
2 Redcar Street,
Southampton SO1 5LL

Edited by David Graves
Typeset by PageMerger, Southampton
Printed in the E.E.C.

British Library Cataloguing in Publication Data

Street, Sean
Petersfield: a pictorial past.
1. Hampshire. Petersfield, history
I. Title
942.2'74

ISBN 1 85455 028 4

Contents

Introduction

"The ancient Borough of Petersfield stands on the very borders of Hants and Sussex, though situated within the former County: and its inhabitants, we think rightly, believe the neighbourhood combines all that is beautiful in the inland scenery of both Counties."

So begins The History of Petersfield, published in 1856 by the Rev. J. Williams, Curate of St. Peter's Church. It was on March 6th, 1857, that the Rev. Williams gave a lecture on the subject, at The National School Rooms, and his little book preserves for us today the main substance of the talk. The National School was in Sussex Road, next to the then vicarage, today known as Heath Lodge. It was demolished some time after 1857. (See Appendix on page 64 for the complete text of Rev. Williams' address.)

Certainly, even now, it would be hard to argue with Williams' praise of the scenic beauty of the area. Nearly a century later, another writer, Brian Vesey-Fitzgerald stood on Butser Hill and saw:

"... below in the green valley between the wooded hills ... Petersfield, and behind in the blue distance, the long line of Hindhead. It is from Old Butser that you should first see Petersfield. Few towns can be viewed so advantageously."

Yet the beauty of the area has always existed very much within the context of the real world, for Petersfield stands, as it were, at a crossroads, and it is true to say that it has always been a point of meeting and rest for travellers as well as a centre for local commerce. In a way, the very presence of the A3 is a sort of metaphor for much of Petersfield's importance through the years. My book looks pictorially at a part of history as it has shown itself through the lenses of cameras and the brushes and pencils of artists who have lived in, or visited the town. In this, the book represents but a fragment of that past; yet it is true to say that, if we but choose to look a little closer, we may find clues to the life of previous generations in buildings and roads which we might usually pass without a second look. Time passes and it becomes increasingly important that we rediscover and remember our past, before it is too late. Where today's Post Office stands, once stood a proud Elizabethan mansion; where the modern Dolphin Court now is, once was the old Post Office, and next to it, the Dolphin Hotel, where, in 1825, William Cobbett stayed, and commented on the reasonable charges; this, in turn became the "County High School for Girls" until its closure in 1960. And could it be that the narrowing of the High Street was a

deliberate act by the early developers of the town, in order to impose a toll point on farmers taking cattle into the Square at its western end, on market days? We leave symptoms of ourselves everywhere. My aim has been to explore some of those symptoms through visual evidence, and to present an affectionate portrait of a Hampshire market town which will, I hope, provide memories for its more senior residents, while giving a sense of the history of the place to those arrived more recently.

Certainly, the town is part of a terrain that has been populated by man from the very earliest times. Indeed, Petersfield Heath, with its famous pond, is perhaps the place to begin any book about the town, for it was here, some six thousand years ago, that some of the earliest inhabitants established themselves.

It is not difficult to understand why the Heath was so attractive; here was a natural clearing, ridges of sand, dry enough to build huts, a good supply of water from the clear, chalk streams, woods full of game, berries and nuts, and flints in the chalk ... the raw material for tools and weapons. The archaeologist Stuart Piggott studied the Heath while at

Churcher's College, and found no less than twenty-one bronze age burial barrows on the Heath, many crowned today with fir trees and dating back to the time of the Pharaohs. Some, known as Bell and Bowl Barrows, were the final resting places of Bronze Age chieftains, while others, the lower "disc" barrows were thought to be the graves of women. Petersfield Heath has been called a sort of Bronze Age "Westminster Abbey" for the surrounding area, and there can be few places in England where so many diverse barrows stand within such a relatively small area.

The same reasons that attracted early man, also brought his successors to Petersfield, and as the town grew outwards from its Norman Church, much of the original Heath became absorbed either for building or for agricultural needs. The fact that it has survived in any form may well be due to its marsh-like characteristics – and of course, to its beauty which is today, as it has been for so long, a magnet to many for miles around.

Having taken into account the undoubted antiquity of the area, it seems strange to refer to Petersfield as a "new town"; yet so it was in the 12th century. Not that this was such an unusual thing at the time. It was a stable and settled period, with trade, prosperity and population growing accordingly. To capitalise on this new-found wealth, many landowners decided that the finest investment they could make in their estates was to build a new town. Such a landowner was the grandson of Henry I, William, Earl of Gloucester, Lord of the Manor of Mapledurham. The Manor had been mentioned in Domesday in these terms:-

"The King holds Mapledurham in lordship. Wulfeva held it; Queen Matilda had it. Before 1066 it answered for 20 hides … Land for 20 ploughs. In lordship 4 ploughs; 34 villagers and 15 smallholders with 15 ploughs … Value of the whole manor before 1066 £25; later and now as much …"

Mapledurham was a large area, and by the time Earl William was ensconced at the beginning of the 12th century, the manor included a wide area of chalk downland, and sandy areas now known as Sheet and Petersfield, as well as Nursted, Weston and Buriton. It is perhaps not without reason that even today, some residents of Buriton smile at the mention of Petersfield's past, rather as an understanding parent smiles at an upstart child. In many ways, Buriton could claim to be the mother of Petersfield. In Earl William's day, these lands were covered by small farms, woods, heath and rough grazing land. Much of it was wasteland, and indeed was well suited to being put to a better use. On this wasteland ('feld') William built his new town. It was in the 12th century that the church was built – St. Peter's – so St. Peter's in the Feld was the natural origin of the town's name. It is hardly surprising that the town should grow from here, and certainly the earliest parts of Petersfield are around the Square and High Street areas. It should be remembered that St. Peter's at this time was still only a chapel, and the Parish remained that of Buriton for many years.

Earl William looked to Winchester for his commercial model for the town, and granted the same rights to the local guild of merchants as existed in the ancient capital. The original charter is lost, but the Earl's widow issued a second in or around the year 1183, confirming these rights:-

"Know all men, present and to come, that I, Hawissa, Countess of Gloucester, have granted and confirmed to my Burgesses of Petersfield who have built and are settled, and who shall build in it, all liberties and free customs in the same Borough which the citizens of Winchester have in their city, who are in a guild of merchants; and let them have the same in a guild of merchants as my husband, William, Earl of Gloucester, granted to them by this charter."

The main industry of Petersfield became wool – hardly surprising considering the fine flocks of sheep that abounded on the downs surrounding the town, and its status was confirmed during the reign of Henry III by its right to a market and two fairs, to be celebrated on the feasts of St. Peter and St. Andrew. The wool trade continued to be a major source of prosperity for a considerable time, possibly reaching its zenith during the 15th and 16th centuries. Out of one industry naturally grew another – the clothing trade – and by the turn of the 16th century, the Town Council was able to proudly declare:-

"The said boroughe heretofore hath maintained one thousand poore people in worke by the trade of Cloathing, without begginge, and hath maintained at publicke charge, besides everie man's private charge, forty men for the service of the realme in the warres."

This may have been a cosmetic attempt to improve an application for borough status, because the population of the Borough at the time was only about 850; thus numbers were probably boosted by including shepherds and allied trades from the surrounding area.

It seems likely that the wool and clothing trades were centred around the area of Petersfield known today as the Spain. Some sources have suggested that the name "The Spain" originally came from the fact that Spanish merchants visited the place, and certainly, much later, in 1810 to be exact, a sale of Spanish sheep did take place there. This point of view is supported by the adjacent "Sheep Street". Others would point to a different derivation – that "Spain" is derived from "Spayne", an old name for

tiles at a time when most buildings were thatched, and to have "Spaynes" was a sign of prosperity.

Certainly "The Spain" had – and still has – tiles in abundance! Regarding "Sheep Street", it has been volunteered that this is a corruption of "Ship Street", referring to a now vanished Inn.

Alongside the growth in the cloth industry, was that of leather and this too reached its peak in Tudor times. There were tanneries near Forebridge and Sheet. It must have been rather unpleasant to have lived in close proximity to the works; ammonia was an important part of the tanning process, and the best source of ammonia was urine. There was also a complaint that workers were polluting local streams, "… and do evacuate and emptie their beasts innards there unto the great annoyance of the inhabitants…"

As well as local industry, the town produced some eminent thinkers, including John Goodyer and John Worlidge. Goodyer, famed as a botanist, was born in Alton in 1592, and, having lived at Droxford for a time, finally made his home in the house that today carries his name, in The Spain.

Until 1932 the west side of The Spain was in the tithing of Weston (Mapledurham), and Goodyer was steward to Sir Thomas Bilson of Mapledurham who gave him the house in which he was living in 1629. While here he made a number of significant botanical discoveries, including his clarifying the four principal types of British elm tree. Both Goodyer and the impressive library of books he built up, became widely known, and visitors came to The Spain from far and wide. He was described by one contemporary as "The ablest Herbarist now living in England", and another noted that "Hee hath an excellent Garden and all kind of Exotick Plants." It is strange and sad to reflect on the fact that "absolutely the chiefest Botanicus in England or Europe" as Goodyer was called by Elias Ashmole, lies, in an unmarked grave, in Buriton churchyard.

John Worlidge was best known for his writings on horticultural and agricultural matters. His best known work was "Systema Agriculturae", which was published in 1669, and which included a Rustic Dictionary of just under 1,000 words. In Worlidge's lifetime, the book went through five editions. He designed a seed drill, although never put it into practice, thereby relinquishing the actual claim to invention to Jethro Tull. He shared with many writers of his time, a prospensity for books with long titles; one such was called:-

Vinetum Britannicum: or a treatise of Cider and Apiarum: or a discourse on Bees: tending to the best way of improving them.

His works apart, little is known of Worlidge's life. He was the great-nephew of John Goodyer, married a lady by the name of Grace, by whom he had a number of children, and became a property owner of some influence. His home was situated at the junction of the High Street and Dragon Street, facing up the High Street. He was Mayor of the Town in 1673, and died on June 29th, 1693. His grave is in St. Peter's Church.

From its very earliest times, it seems likely that Petersfield was at the intersection of important roads – although in the beginning these would have been no more than tracks – and as the years passed, its position geographically became more significant.

Carrier services connected the town with Southampton, and as the importance of Portsmouth grew as a naval base, so Petersfield's importance grew with it. When, in the first part of the 16th century the fleet was being built up to strength the strategic worth of the route was reflected in the increased traffic and the various services needed to cater for that traffic. Thus the town became a natural resting place for travellers and their horses, a fact made all the more necessary, since many of the routes in and out of the town meant a stiff climb, and therefore weary men and animals. To accommodate this trade, the early 1600's saw a good number of inns offering rest and refreshment, among them The White Hart, Anchor, George, Swan, Red Lion, Green Dragon, Three Horseshoes and the Crown.

Many distinguished – and some infamous – visitors came to the town, en route from London to Portsmouth, and thence, often, overseas. Charles II came through the town twice, in 1668 and 1671; indeed, he may well have visited Petersfield on other occasions during his travels. Samuel Pepys is known to have stayed here on several occasions, and a much cherished local story is that he played bowls while a guest at the old White Hart, which was situated in the High Street, where Winton House now stands. On May 1st, 1661, Pepys tells us in his Diary:

"Up early, and baited at Petersfield, in the Room which the King lay in lately, at his being there. Here very merry, and played with our wives at bowls."

On May 3rd, presumably on his way home, he mentions another visit:

"Took coach to Petersfield … Here my wife and I lay in the room the Queen lately lay, at her going into France."

He came to Petersfield at least twice more, on one occasion in 1668 to meet Sir Thomas Allin with last minute instructions for a Mediterranean voyage. Then in 1683, on his way to embark at Portsmouth for Cadiz, Pepys stayed again in the town.

Stylish as Samuel Pepys was, another 17th century visitor must have made a greater impression on local people; for in 1698, Peter the Great stayed for a night in Petersfield, on his way to Portsmouth to watch naval fleet manoeuvres. By all accounts, he was greatly annoyed by the way the natives of the town stared at him. With his wild appearance, and considerable retinue, the locals could hardly be blamed for their awed incredulity! The White Hart was Petersfield's most important inn during the 17th and 18th century, and the bowling green would have been at the rear, a garden, meadows where the main car park now stands, and with stables close by.

Visitors brought income for the locals, but they also brought the risk of disease, and during the latter part of the 16th century sickness and famine struck Petersfield, increasing the annual death-rate dramatically. At the same time, standards of living – at least, for some residents – had begun to improve, and these improvements increased further with house chimneys and the arrival of glass for windows. Having said that, these were no protection when, in the 1660's, the Great Plague was carried to Hampshire by travellers from London, and more than two hundred people died in the town. Of those who perished, the first mentioned in the church register is one Thomas Trimmer, who died in 1666, of whom it is said:

"This was the first man that died of that most fatall plague that happened in this towne the year above written; he was buried April 5th."

Samuel Pepys, writing in his Diary on April 4th, 1667, commented that:

"One at table told an odd passage of this late plague; that at Petersfield I think, he said, one side of the Street had every house almost infected through the town, and the other not one shut up."

It is interesting to note that, although the Plague was at its peak in London in 1665, it was not until the following year that towns like Petersfield felt the full force of it.

Another "plague" which grew as a result of travel was that of road-side robbery; attacks by highwaymen became rife during the seventeenth century, and by December, 1692, official rewards for capture were being offered in such papers as the London Gazette:

"Whereas His Majesty hath been this day informed by the PostMaster-General that the Mails going to Portsmouth have been robbed, viz on Saturday the 10th of this instant at twelve a'clock in the night by five persons well mounted and armed between Petersfield and Portsmouth; and on Tuesday the thirteenth instant at seven a'clock at night by three men well mounted and armed between Alton and Petersfield; His Majesty is graciously pleased to promise that there shall be a reward of two hundred pounds forthwith paid by the Right Honourable the Lords Commissioners of the Treasury to such person or persons as shall apprehend any one of the said persons who robbed or assisted in robbing the said Mails…"

Petersfield has had its share of great and powerful families and one of the most influential seems to have been the Bilsons. Sir Thomas Bilson lived at Mapledurham House, which was swept away when the railways arrived. He was Sheriff of Hampshire in 1651, and when James II became King, Bilson was one of two local M.P.s. Bilson's mother lived in the Elizabethan-built Castle House, on the West side of the Square; this beautiful building was demolished in 1913 to make way for new developments. The Midland Bank and main Post Office now occupy the site.

In July, 1703, Queen Anne visited Petersfield on her way to Portsmouth. It was just over a year since the death of her husband, and she may have taken the opportunity of thanking the town for its message of condolence of March 1702:-

"To the Queen's Most Excellent Majesty. The humble Address of the Mayor and Burgesses of Your Majesty's ancient Borough of Petersfield in the County of Southampton, together with the rest of the Gentlemen and Inhabitants of the said Borough.

May it please your Majesty, We Your Majesty's most Dutiful and Loyal Subjects, pray leave to Condole with Your Majesty for the exstream loss of our late most Gracious Sovereign King William the Third (of blessed memory) whose Death, considering the Glorious Designs of that Great Prince, would not only fill these Nations, but likewise all Europe, to whom Liberty is precious, with insupportable affliction, did not Your Majesty's Royal Qualifications and happy Accession to the Throne entirely relieve us: Upon which Occasion we beseech Your Majesty to accept of this our most hearty congratulation, and with the utmost Zeal and Duty to assure Your Majesty, we are firmly resolved to contribute all that is Valuable to us for the Defence of Your Majesty's most Sacred Person and Government, which we pray God Almighty long to preserve."

With what care, and with how much soul-searching for the right word, must that address have been written!

By the 1730's, the great family in the town was that of the Jolliffe's. They built Petersfield House, now gone, which stood close to where the present Police Station now stands in St. Peter's Road. In those days this was called "New Way". It was under the will of Sir William Jolliffe that the Statue of William III – arguably Petersfield's most familiar landmark – was set up. The Jolliffes had come to power through finance and trade, a success they shared with the Gibbon family of Buriton. The two families met in political confrontation in the General Election of 1734, when Sir William defeated Edward Gibbon the second by just twenty votes. The Gibbons were, however, to gain fame elsewhere, for Edward Gibbon the third was to become immortal as a writer, in particular as author of "The Decline and Fall of the Roman Empire." Indeed, the historian himself was persuaded, albeit reluctantly, to stand for the Petersfield seat in the Election of 1761. Edward had been educated in Switzerland, and served in the Hampshire militia during the Seven Years' War. His diary clearly shows lack of interest in the election campaign, and his relief at not being returned as a Member!

"March 22nd, 1761. I got down to Beriton where I was to engage in a contested election. Some free-holders of Petersfield had persuaded my father to stand against Jolliffe's interest, upon the supposition he could not transfer any of his votes having settled them upon his wife. My father declined in my favor. I had never any opinion of the affair and was only comforted by the reflexion that it cost hardly any thing. One Barnard of Alresford, made me lose the Election or rather gave me an opportunity of giving it up with honour."

It was the time of the Rotten Boroughs, and Petersfield was known for a while as one of the most rotten of them all! Members were returned to Parliament as a result of the total control they held over the voting population, which often consisted of simply family, friends and those chosen by prospective candidates.

The amount of fine surviving Georgian architecture in Petersfield is evidence that during the 18th century, prosperity returned in some measure to the town, after a considerable time of lying fallow. Although Daniel Defoe, who stayed here during the 1720's found Petersfield's hostelries to be the most interesting aspect of the place, describing it as "a town eminent for little but its being full of good inns."

During this time, in 1729, one of the town's proudest educational establishments, Churcher's College, came into being. Richard Churcher was an East India Merchant, and he founded the College with £3,000 as a bluecoat charity school in premises which still stand in the road to which it gave its name – College Street. The purpose, as originally stated was to establish

"… a College … for boys to be taken out of, and belonging to the borough of Petersfield … whose parents would give security to the Trustees, to oblige their sons to be bound apprentices to Masters of ships making their voyages to the East Indies."

However, by the latter part of the 19th century, the establishment had grown beyond all original expectations, and new premises were built on Ramshill, where today, the College continues to expand and develop. Sport has always been well supported at the College; there is an amusing piece of period press reporting in the Churcher's archives regarding a football match, dated November 17th, 1894:-

"The Petersfield and Chichester clubs were to have met on the Heath on Saturday, but for some unaccountable reason, Chichester failed to put in an appearance, although the home team were on the ground, ready to try conclusions with them… Failing the arrival of the proper opponents, a game with the Churcher's College team, including three masters, was arranged, and proved a very capital exhibition."

Staying on the subject of sport, eight years after Richard Churcher had founded his college, a man was born who was to become a much renowned figure in Petersfield … indeed in Hampshire, and one might justifiably say in all England. For it was in 1737, that John Small arrived in the world. He started his working life as a humble shoemaker, but was to be one of the founder members of the famous Hambledon Cricket team. He spent eighty-four of his eighty-nine years in Petersfield, and, on the day of a match, would walk to the Hambledon ground. He lived at No. 12, The High Street, and here set up a business making cricket bats and balls. He was also a silk mercer and draper. His sign advertised:

"John Small will make bat and ball, pitch a wicket, play at cricket with any man in England."

On one famous occasion, in a match between Hambledon and All England, John Small carried his bat to the end of an innings that lasted three days.

He was also a fine musician; when he was fourteen years old, he played the bass viol in the Petersfield choir, and continued as a member for seventy-five years, playing the tenor violin without glasses until within a year of his death. The stories surrounding him are legion, and perhaps one of the best tells of how he saved his life by playing the violin to an angry bull; he was crossing a field with a friend when the bull attacked them. John began to play, the bull stopped and listened, and both men escaped unharmed.

John Small died in 1826, and lies buried with his family in Petersfield Churchyard. The well-known poem, composed in his memory is not on his stone, although it is probably in the hearts of many Hampshire cricket lovers!

"Here lies, bowl'd out by Death's unerring ball,
A cricketer renowned, by name John Small.
But though his name was Small yet great
  his fame,
For nobly did he play the 'noble game'.
His life was like an innings, long and good,
Full ninety summers he had Death withstood,
At length the ninetieth winter came, when (fate
Not leaving him one solitary mate),
This last of Hambledonians, old John Small,
Gave up his bat and ball, his leather,
  wax and all."

It may be that several John Small legends have become intertwined, because, indeed, there have been a number of John Smalls in Petersfield, four in succession to be precise; the first came from Empshott, and lived at 22, The High Street, where he set up business as a saddler cordwainer. The second, the famous cricketer, was succeeded by a third, who later moved to 8, The Square, and continued in business as a silk mercer, a trade that was continued by the fourth John Small.

There is another reference to Petersfield and cricket in the writings, of all people, of Gilbert White, author of the famed "Natural History of Selborne". In a letter, dated August 1st, 1787, White mentions that his nephew,

"Little Tom Clement is visiting at Petersfield, where he plays much at cricket: Tom bats, his grand-father bowls, and his great-grandmother watches out!"

In 1787, John Small would have been a mere fifty years old, so it is not beyond the bounds of possibility that young Tom Clement had come under the great man's spell!

The 18th and 19th centuries saw Petersfield moving towards its peak as a staging post, which had well and truly arrived by 1830, when thirty coaches a day stopped for refreshment here, thus continuing a thread which has existed through history, and which, with the railway and commuter traffic, continues today.

Although, as has been said, a number of monarchs have stayed in, or passed through Petersfield, there is apparently no direct connection between the town and the King with whom it is most associated in popular imagination:- William III. When Sir William Jolliffe left £500 for the erection of the statue in 1749, King William must have been something of a symbol of Protestant stability, and worth immortalising, lest the people forget. The statue was first placed in New Way (St. Peter's Road) opposite the Jolliffe's residence. Originally it was a golden horse, being guilded, although cast in lead by John Cheere, who produced famous work of this kind during the mid-18th century from his yards near Hyde Park Corner in London. It owes its origin to the inspiration of a statue in Rome of Marcus Aurelius, but its more immediate lineage comes from Hull, in the shape of Peter Scheemakers' statue of William, cast in bronze. Petersfield House was demolished in 1793, and in 1815, William III was moved to his present position in The Square. There, it sank into decay until 1911, when the District Council took charge of it. Public subscription raised the necessary funds for its restoration, and in 1913, in a ceremony chronicled pictorially later in this book, William re-emerged in his full glory to face the twentieth century. Present at the unveiling were members of the Dutch navy, and a number of Orangemen. It was a great public show of affection for Petersfield's adopted monarch.

The statue has not been without its controversy, however. It has been called "a magnificent, heroic work", but on the other hand, Brian Vesey-Fitzgerald was less complimentary, writing in 1949 he said:-

"Quite the most ridiculous statue in England. I can only imagine that Petersfield keeps it because they know in the town that they have something that you would see equalled nowhere else in the world… Poor Dutch William! He was altogether too dignified to deserve such a guying, unconscious guying though it undoubtedly was."

For all Vesey-Fitzgerald's attacks, the statue of William III in the Square remains a much-loved centrepiece for the town, and certainly it is difficult to imagine Petersfield without it today.

The Petersfield area has quite alot to be proud of architecturally; the Victorian architect, Sir Arthur Blomfield was responsible for the building of the churches at East Liss and Sheet, as well as the sadly abandoned building at Privett, the spire of which has been for so long a landmark in the Meon Valley. In 1873, Blomfield also restored Petersfield Church itself; anyone who is in any doubt as to the meaning of the phrase "Victorian Gothic" should visit the church, and look at the pulpit. It was designed by Blomfield, and is as good an example as may be found anywhere. Indeed, this style, which Blomfield championed, is evident in much of his work locally.

If the Gothic was an influence for Blomfield, then for W.F. Unsworth and H. Inigo Triggs, the inspiration came from Norman Shaw and William Morris and others in the Arts and Crafts Movement. It was Unsworth and Triggs who were responsible in 1911 for the building and grounds known as

Ashford Chace, close to the Shoulder of Mutton Hill, on the Ashford Estate. The Estate had been bought by N.C. and A.S. Graham on behalf of their brother-in-law, the Naturalist, Artist and Explorer, Aubyn Bernard Rochfort Trevor-Battye. Triggs was a great garden designer, and paved the way for the subsequent development of the grounds. Trevor-Battye spent little time here, however, and so let the house to Sir Thomas Horder in 1920. In 1924, Horder, King George V's chief Physician, bought the house and about 120 acres of land for £11,000. For many years he expanded the grounds and gardens with great love and care, until his death, in 1955. Some of that care may be judged in the photographs contained in this book, showing the grounds at their peak. It was these grounds that for many years provided the home of the Steep Shakespeare Players, who performed there until 1961, and whose reputation stretched far and wide. It has to be said that the proposal to build Ashford Chace – William Morris – influenced or otherwise – did not meet with the approval of the poet, Edward Thomas, who was living in the cottage adjacent to the building site, and who much prefered the meadow that had been there before. William Morris and his contemporaries were also an influence in the building and philosophy of Bedales school at Steep, at which two of Edward Thomas's children were pupils. G.H. Lupton was responsible for much building in the Morris tradition at the school, outstandingly, the Lupton Hall built in 1913, and the Memorial Library (1921). In the building of the latter he was assisted by another great craftsman of the area, Edward Barnsley, whose woodwork is prized the world over. Bedales was founded in 1893 in Sussex by J.H. Badley, known to Bedalians as "The Chief", and was one of the first "Progressive" schools, aiming to free itself from some of the bad effects of the traditional English Public School system. Certainly it was innovative in its introduction of residential co-education, small classes and a close relationship between staff and pupils. To visit the school today is to experience still a feeling of refreshment.

Above all, the artist most associated with Petersfield is Flora Twort, one of the great characters of the town for many years, from her arrival in 1918, after spending her early life, first in Cornwall and then London, where her father worked for the Inland Revenue. She was born in 1893, and lived into her 90's. Her famous studio was at numbers 1 and 2, The Square, and these premises she let to Gilbert and Stanley Spencer while she was studying at the Slade School of Art. In the pages of this book, she is seen at work on a portrait of Lord Horder. This was commissioned to hang in the Royal College of Surgeons building in Lincoln's Inn Fields. There is a nice story attached to this, which tells how she had wanted for some time to have him as a subject, but, although they were good friends, she did not feel able to approach him on the subject. It subsequently transpired that he had been slightly offended that she hadn't asked him to sit! Her studios were popular as a book, card and gift shop. ("It was always the place to go if you wanted something really nice … something of quality!" as one long-standing resident once told me.) Flora worked in pencil, pastel, brush and charcoal. Curiously, for an artist so much associated with drawing and painting place, her great love was portraiture. Yet it is the Petersfield she saw and left for us in her pictures we remember, notably her famous studies of The Square, and of the Heath Fair. Her hope was that the Town should use her house as a permanent home for her pictures. Certainly she is one of Petersfield's human traditions, and will rightly remain so.

Any story of a town must also be about people, and no where more so than at Petersfield. For the place never existed in isolation, if anywhere ever can; the village hinterland brought farmers and other locals to market and to the fair for centuries, and it still does. Lime kilns and an ancient glass-making factory at Buriton, brick works at Liss, (my Great Grandfather built his house at West Liss from bricks made in his own works), and sheep on the downs. Through history, industry provided work for hands skilled in the wool and cloth trade, in leather work, and in 1919, in rubber products at the ITS works in Sandringham Road. This has in turn now vanished, and the emphasis shifts once more, but essentially the balance continues to be maintained between a town for travellers, a market, and local industry. As the twenty first century approaches, the preservation of the true essence of Petersfield becomes more critical and more crucial. As the photographs and drawings in this book show, much of the past remains as our heritage, but much has also been swept away. Such is progress, but it is the way in which the needs of the present and the future is confronted that is so crucial. How civic dignitaries from the past would have felt, had they known that the arches and columns of their old Town Hall in the Square would be preserved as the facade of a Gentlemen's lavatory, can only be guessed at! However, at least the arches and columns survive.

Such continuity tells us something of the town and its history. It also tells us something of the people who walked its streets before us. With the help of a little imagination, I hope my book and the pictures in it may act as a guide into the past of Petersfield and the villages that surround it. An awareness of the importance of Place and Community may well be one of the most valuable treasures we can take into the 21st century. We cannot hope to develop that awareness until we have an understanding of our local history, and how it relates to us today. Flora Twort saw a landscape, but she saw it with figures in it. For myself, I still see the town and the countryside my great grandfather knew, as he drove into Petersfield from his brick works at West Liss, or later, from his farm at East Meon, and although he would undoubtedly notice change, there is much he would recognise too. There is an essence to a place that remains, a quality I attempted to capture in a book of poems of the South Country entitled "A Walk in Winter".

"Walk in any road, on any path, there is the
   salty taste
of living lingering on earth's tongue …
world a merchant's yard, full of crash and shout,
the savoury essence of hands' work,
life's job being done, going on continually.
So the shipwright and carpenter, farmer
   and clerk
with tool and thought hold themselves up
   to time,
printing a being on future years,
a richness that colours light parchment.
Even in silence the air is left ringing."

Let us listen for the whispers of the past amid the 'crash and shout' of the present. In doing so, we may well be preserving our future.

1. The Square, Petersfield

The Square. The focal point of Petersfield life as it looked for much of the 19th century. The buildings in front of the church were removed in the 1890s. Clearly seen in this picture is the passageway through the buildings – under the circular windows – which used to lead directly to the churchyard. *(Petersfield Society)*

Castle House. This fine house dominated The Square from Tudor times until it was demolished in 1913. Many great names associated with the town lived here, among them John Bonham Carter. The last years of the house were as a boys school. Throughout the First World War, the site lay barren, the present Post Office being built there in 1922. *(Petersfield Society)*

16

with Castle House at the turn of the century. The statue of William III was by this time in a very poor state of
n 1911 the council took it under its aegis, and in 1913, fully restored, it was the centre-piece of great
ion. *(Hants Museums Service)*

Castle House Garden. A view of lost
Edwardian tranquillity. This lawn has
been claimed, erroneously, to be the site
of what is known as "Pepys' Bowling
Green". If indeed Samuel Pepys did play
bowls in Petersfield, it would not have
been here. As the lawn of the boys
school, however, it is certain that the site
saw much fun and games of its own!
(Petersfield Society)

The Square in the latter years of the 19th century. The Old Town Hall was demolished in 1898. The schoolboy in the right foreground may well be from Castle House. To his right, just visible, is the drinking fountain which may now be seen in the central car park. *(Hants Museums Service)*

No. 1, The Square. A lovely Tudor building which, for many years, had its glories concealed beneath plasterwork. It was once a farm house belonging to Castle House, and has had a number of identities since. From the 1920s until the 1950s, it was well known as an arts and craft shop, run by the artist, Flora Twort, together with Marie Brahms and Hester Wagstaff. *(Petersfield Society)*

Square *c.*, 1905. It is market day, and the scene is one virtually unchanged through the centuries. There is a theory that the High Street's narrow top was designed as a toll point for farmers entering the Square on market day. The last cattle market was held here in 1962. *(Hants Museums Service)*

Postcard of the Square from the Church Tower. It dates from before 1914 judging from the fact that the first co-op building, built in 1914, does not appear in this picture (the old public house is still standing next to the Corn Exchange on the right of the Square). This is the nearest thing to an aerial view of Edwardian Petersfield we have! As to the Corn Exchange building, this was built in 1866, and has served a number of purposes, including at one time a concert hall.
(Petersfield Society)

Hants and Dorset Bus 1926, in The Square. It has come from Southampton, via Bishops Waltham, and judging by the tyres, the passengers must have felt every bump in the road! *(Hants Museums Service)*

THE 'DOLPHIN' HOTEL,
PETERSFIELD.

THE ACCOMMODATION COMPRISES:

Coffee, Smoking, Writing and Reading Rooms

Drawing & Private Sitting Rooms.

Ball Room.   Billiards.

STABLING FOR 40 HORSES.

LARGE COVERED YARD AND LOCK-UP COACH-HOUSE.

Good Cuisine and Well-Selected Wines.

MODERATE CHARGES.

Posting in all its Branches.

The Square during the 1930s. At the time of writing this book, plans were afoot to cease the parking of cars on the actual Square itself; quite rightly, for The Square is still the focus of Petersfield life, and the presence of the car enhances it as little now as then! *(Petersfield Society)*

The Church during the 1940s. Probably a war-time picture, judging by the "Wings For Victory" poster. The strange and unsitely erection in front of the church was an air-raid shelter. *(Petersfield Society)*

The Square in the early 1900s. Compare this photograph with earlier views; it is possible to identify the pillars and stone adornments that once graced the old town hall and the other buildings that once fronted the Church.

2. Education

Churcher's College, Petersfield

Churcher's Old College. Founded in 1729 as a bluecoat charity school by Richard Churcher, these premises still dominate College Street, which owes its name to them. It was in 1882 that Churcher's moved to its present site, a Victorian Gothic building on Ramshill.

Churcher's College. Taken when the College's present building was new. By the time of its move, its original aim, to prepare pupils for work in the East India Service, had long since changed. It has a distinguished record today in the professions and the services. *(Hants Museums Service)*

Heath Harrison House, Churcher's College.
This fine house was presented to Churcher's in
1932 by Sir Heath Harrison, Bart., and is
traditionally the Head Master's residence.
(Street)

Princess Beatrice
inspecting the Guard of
Honour of Churcher's
College Officer Training
Corps at the Bicentenary
Bazaar, December 13th,
1922. According to the
College Magazine, The
Churcherian, the Bazaar
raised just under £200 for
the improvement fund.
(Churcher's College)

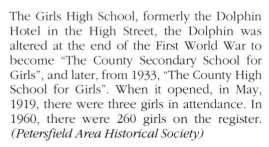

The Girls High School, formerly the Dolphin
Hotel in the High Street, the Dolphin was
altered at the end of the First World War to
become "The County Secondary School for
Girls", and later, from 1933, "The County High
School for Girls". When it opened, in May,
1919, there were three girls in attendance. In
1960, there were 260 girls on the register.
(Petersfield Area Historical Society)

The County High School for Girls. The Library and (below) the Art Room during the 1940s. The School was closed in the early 1960s, and Dolphin Court now stands on the site. Do you recognise any faces in these pictures? *(Petersfield Area Historical Society)*

Bedales School under construction *c.*, 1903. J.H. Badley founded Bedales in 1893 in Sussex; the school moved to its present Victorian House at the turn of the century. A purpose-built block was added, the first of many alterations that have developed the school's physical structure to accommodate its educational growth. *(Bedales School)*

Dunhurst. The junior department of Bedales, shortly after its opening. (Note the size of the trees.) Helen Thomas, wife of the poet, Edward, taught here for a while. *(Bedales School)*

Building Bedales Library (left). The man in the picture is Geoffrey Lupton, a noted furniture maker who has left his mark indelibly on, not only Bedales, but on the surrounding area. He was a disciple of William Morris and an Old Bedalian. *(Bedales School)*

Inside the Library (below). The Morris tradition of the library design is clear in this picture. Although it appears older, it was in fact built in 1919-20 as a War Memorial. There is a tradition … maintained strictly … of silence and unsupervised study. In a 1958 edition of the Hampshire Magazine, a pupil is reported as saying "I think it is the most religious place in the school." The central stone fireplace has since been removed. *(Bedales School)*

Exterior of the Library today. It was finished in 1921. "Despite its rule of silence," wrote one Old Bedalian, "the library was quite a social milieu: eye contact and note-writing went on, and its rather open structure with a balcony level made it quite a theatre." *(Street)*

Petersfield National School. The National School was in Sussex Road, next door to the vicarage, which became known as Heath Lodge and is now redeveloped as retirement flats. It is possible that the school used buildings left over from the 18th century, when a Mr. Patrick had a brewhouse in the area. It was demolished some time after 1875.

PETERSFIELD NATIONAL SCHOOLS.

Hants and Sussex News,

PETERSFIELD, MAY 22, 1901.

Educational.

LADIES' COLLEGE, High-street, Petersfield. Principal, Miss HENSON.—Pupils receive a Good Education, with careful attention to health and domestic comfort, on moderate terms. Preparation for Examinations if desired. Hitherto every Candidate sent successful. Summer term commences May 6th.

Miss Henson's School, 1903. The Misses Henson, Fanny and Susan ran the school until its closure, at about the time this photograph was taken. Susan Henson is in the centre of the group; she is flanked by two other teachers, Miss 'Flo' on her right, and Miss Wickham, the married sister of Susan, on her left. It was at 24, High Street on a site now occupied by an insurance brokers. It is possible that the premises had been a school "for young ladies of the upper classes" from as early as the 1830s. The Henson sisters' mother set up her school around 1861.
(Petersfield Area Historical Society)

3. Celebrations, Relaxation

Steep Shakespeare Players. For many years, until 1961, the Steep Shakespeare Players performed at Ashford Chace, home of Lord Horder. The idyllic setting and fine productions brought them fame far beyond the village, and performances are still remembered fondly today. *(Petersfield Society)*

Site of Steep Shakespeare Players productions. The building was used as a dressing room for productions. The beauty of Ashford Chace as a setting for the productions is clear from this tranquil picture. *(Petersfield Society)*

The Heath Pond from the air. This picture, possibly taken during the 1920s is a rare, early example of aerial photography. The Pond itself covers some twenty two acres. The Heath shows evidence of human habitation during the time of the Pharaohs. *(Petersfield Society)*

Bathing at the Heath Pond. The pond is not shown on Isaac Taylor's map of Hampshire, published in 1759, but is clearly marked on another map, published in 1813. However, it is a well documented fact that water was always there, if just below the surface; on one occasion, workmen had to run for their lives as water welled up as they were digging sand. The land was always marshy, and in the eighteenth century farm cattle actually drowned in such conditions, and it was the farmers who decided that a lake would be safer. It is man, rather than nature, who must be thanked for one of Petersfield's best-loved amenities! Prior to the acquisition of much of the Heath by the Urban District Council in 1913, a number of aristocratic local families had boat houses on the Pond. *(Petersfield Society)*

Unveiling the statue. In 1912 the statue of William III was moved to the Square from its original site in St. Peter's Road. It fell into decay, but was restored in 1913. On September 3rd, "In brilliant sunshine", Lord Selborne "without the slightest hitch", pulled a lever and revealed the statue, festooned with laurel and decorated with orange bows. *(Petersfield Society)*

Lord Selborne, (standing, holding hat, gloves and umbrella) has just unveiled the statue, untying lines attached to the post in front of him. Standing to his right, holding notes, is H. Inigo Triggs, co-designer of Ashford Chace. *(Petersfield Society)*

The Moment of Unveiling. The crowd included the scarlet-clad Territorial Force of the Hampshire Regiment, the local fire brigade, and Orangemen in full regalia. As the Union flags fell away from the statue, the Square rang with cheers, the church bells rang, the soldiers presented arms, and the band struck up the national anthem. *(Petersfield Society)*

Welcome Inn. The Welcome Inn, which was situated in Station Road. This picture, taken shortly after its opening in 1940, shows its predecessor, The Volunteer Arms on the left. Throughout the war years, The Welcome Inn was the headquarters of the Local Observer Corps. *(Petersfield Society)*

The same site, nearly fifty years on. In 1989, I was just in time to photograph the old Inn sign-post, surrounded by a new development of "starter homes".

Warship Week, 1942. A great fund-raising event for the War effort, Petersfield's Warship Week was held from February 28th-March 7th, 1942. On the first day, the Churcher's College contingent of the J.T.C. and band led the way to the Square through the streets of the town. *(Churcher's College)*

Hunt at Bereleigh House, south of Privett. The hounds belong to the Hambledon Hunt, and the meet is taking place in about 1925. At the end of the First World War, Bereleigh was auctioned and its new owner became Major Reginald Nicholson. In the photograph, Major Nicholson is to be seen in the background, wearing the tall top hat and full hunting regalia. *(Standfield)*

Petersfield Fair. The Fair on the Heath held on October 6th dates back seven centuries. Fairs on the feast days of St. Peter and St. Andrew were granted by William de Clare in 1255. Once, the horse fair was a major part of this annual event. It was known as the "Taro" Fair; one explanation for the name was that in former times, Welsh dealers brought cattle and ponies to sell here; the word "Taro" being a command shouted by the drovers to persuade the animals to move. Another possibility is that "Taro" was a shout of triumph on completing a deal. Today, the emphasis is on family fun and entertainment. *(Petersfield Society)*

4. The Commercial Round

Removal of Garage Signs. Probably Dragon Street, Petersfield. The Petersfield Society has for many years been a watchdog over the town's urban environment. The Society was formed in 1945 with the avowed intent of "conserving and promoting what is visually important in the town and its surrounding countryside", a role it continues to fulfil actively, today. In this picture, unsightly signs, so much a part of the twentieth century, are being cleared. *(Petersfield Society)*

The old Co-operative building. The old Co-operative building was built in about 1914, and replaced an Inn that had stood on the site for centuries. This photograph was taken during the Second World War. The building was later replaced by the present Co-op. *(Petersfield Society)*

East Meon Forge. The picture is Edwardian, perhaps about 1908. In front of the wagon, with a hammer in his hand, is the blacksmith, Jim Hobbs, with his sons on either side. *(Standfield)*

East Meon Forge today. Times change, and the requirements of society change too, but there is a continuity of purpose shown in this modern picture of the same establishment. *(Stan Smith)*

ITS Rubber, 1920s. ITS Rubber, in Sandringham Road, Petersfield, was founded in 1919 for the purpose of making the "Concave-Convex" shoe heel, under licence from an American firm. The factory closed in 1987, and the site is now a housing estate. *(Hants Record Office)*

West Meon Railway Viaduct. The viaduct, which spanned the West Meon/East Meon Road, carrying the Meon Valley Railway line on its way, was made up of seven hundred tons of steel, on concrete bases. *(Hants Record Office)*

Labourers engaged in building the Meon Valley Railway line during the early 1900s. The line ran the 22½ miles from Alton to Fareham, and 600 workers like these men worked for sixpence an hour to build it. It opened in 1903, and the last passenger train ran on February 5th, 1955. *(Hants Record Office)*

The 'Middy' as it was affectionately known ran from Petersfield to Midhurst and provided a valuable service, much missed when it closed on 7th February 1955.
(Lens of Sutton)

Petersfield Junction *c.*, 1953. The station first opened around 1859 as part of the final link in the London-Petersfield line built by the L.S.W.R. Petersfield Station has a twin in Godalming, they were constructed to the same design. *(Lens of Sutton)*

Rogate and Harting Station. The branch line to Midhurst was opened in 1864 by the Petersfield Railway Company. This station, a classic country affair, was later renamed, more simply, Rogate. There was also a station at Elsted. Closed to passenger traffic in 1955, the goods yard stayed open for business until 1969.
(Lens of Sutton)

21-23 High St. This elegant 18th century house was, from 1900, the home of A.W. Childs Ltd., printers of "The Hants and Sussex News", better known to some as "The Squeaker". The printing works was at the rear, and the shop itself was a bookshop and stationers. The building was demolished in 1964. A supermarket now occupies the site. *(Petersfield Society)*

These shops, on the corner of The Avenue and Dragon Street are seen as they were in the 1940s. The building dates from the 18th century. *(Petersfield Society)*

Charcoal burning on the Ashford Estate (above). The size of the burners can be judged by making a comparison with the workman in the centre foreground of the picture. *(Petersfield Society)*

Flora Twort. A well known Petersfield figure, seen here at work on the portrait of another, Lord Horder, the owner of Ashford Chace.
(Hants Museums Service)

5. Petersfield Streets

Map of Petersfield 1922. Hester Wagstaff, the artist responsible for this map of the town, was a colleague of Flora Twort. The map is an interesting study of Petersfield, showing as it does aspects of the town now gone forever. Most obvious of these is the area behind the High Street, now the central car park.

Top of Sheep Street. 25, The Square. This house, for many years remembered as a book shop in the old style, is now a part of a modern solicitor's office.
(*Petersfield Society*)

Goodyers, in The Spain, proudly bears a plaque stating it was once the home of the botanist, John Goodyer. Today, his botanical library is housed in Magdalene College, Oxford, and is increasingly valued as a great source of information by modern botanists.
(Petersfield Society)

Spain House. The title of "The Spain" has caused much controversy over the years. It has been said that the area owes its name to the sale of Spanish wool. In medieval times, it was called "Le Green". Most likely is the explanation that this, as a district of quality was known by the fact that houses here were tiled rather than thatched. The old word for a tile was a "Spayne". The house, apparently eighteenth century, is now divided as flats. *(Petersfield Society)*

Antrobus Alms Houses (right and below). In the 1620s, William Antrobus left money to build these alms houses. Unfortunately, there was not enough to set up an alms trust as well, so their maintenance was always something of a struggle. In the early part of the twentieth century, they fell into disrepair, and these pictures show their last years. The first picture was taken during the 1930s, while the second, judging by the air-raid siren in the distance, was clearly taken during the Second World War. The alms houses stood in College Street. *(Petersfield Society)*

The Jubilee Committee   *Midsummer 1887*

To LEWIS A. B. COLE,
STATIONER & NEWSAGENT,
PETERSFIELD.
Next the CORN-EXCHANGE.

1887

Sheep Street. The name may well be misleading. Originally, it was probably "Ship" street, taking the name from a well-known "Ship" that sailed there until the nineteenth century, "The Royal George" public house! *(Petersfield Society)*

Sheep Street in Edwardian days. An image of ancient England, often romanticised; it is pleasing to note how well the character of the street has been preserved today.

High Street, probably in the mid-nineteenth century. Cole's Repository (on the right) was run by Joseph Cole, who lived here from 1841. He was stationer, newsagent, bookseller, tobacconist and perfumier, as well as a hairdresser. One of his charges was to cut the hair of the boys of Churcher's College, then in College Street.

High Street, North Side, looking East. The building in the centre of the photograph is Winton House, which stands on the site of an old inn, the White Hart. It was here that Samuel Pepys was reputed to have stayed, and played bowls in a garden at the rear. *(Petersfield Society)*

High Street. This picture may well date from about 1900. In the distance, we see that Castle House is still intact, and on the left, that the old Post Office, built in 1892, is still operating. In 1919, the Dolphin Hotel became the Girls High School, and stayed as such until 1960, when it and the old Post Office, which had been converted to a Doctors' practice in 1922, were demolished. *(Hants Museums Service)*

Nos. 17-19, High Street. One of Petersfield's most distinguished buildings, in terms of history. Petersfield's first known printer, Thomas Willmer, operating from here, served Churcher's College in its early days. It was originally a Tudor House, renovated by Nicholas Patience in 1613, during which time the chimney was probably added. It is best known today by the name of the cafe, "The Punch and Judy". *(Petersfield Society)*

Mould's, the Undertakers. Mould's were on the corner of Dragon Street and St. Peter's Road. This picture dates from between the wars; the cafe in the picture was also owned by members of the Mould family. *(Petersfield Society)*

Bottom of High Street. The writer on agriculture and horticulture, John Worlidge lived in a house on this site. This photograph may well have been taken during – or just after – the war. *(Petersfield Society)*

Today, the soldier has gone, and there is more traffic, but otherwise, the scene is curiously unchanged.

Dragon House, Dragon St. Architecturally, the house is a curious mixture of styles. Parts of it date back to Tudor times, although the facade is undeniably Regency. During the 18th century, it was the home of the well-known brewing family, the Patricks. *(Petersfield Society)*

Heath House. The house, built on an ancient site on Sussex Road, was probably mostly 18th century. During the war it served as a hospital for evacuees. Thereafter it was allowed to decline, and was demolished during the late 1950s. *(Petersfield Society)*

Ancient Barrow on Petersfield Heath. This burial mound, near Heath Road, photographed in 1938, is a part of one of Britain's most important collections of sand-based burial mounds. In total, there are twenty one barrows on the Heath, dating from the Bronze Age, about 1,500 B.C. There is, however, evidence of man being here between 5,000 and 2,000 B.C., making this the oldest site of human habitation yet discovered in Eastern Hampshire.

Lavant Street looking towards the station at the turn of the century. In its early days, during the late 19th century, Lavant Street presented an aspect of middle class residential respectability. The coming of the car - and the commercial world - has changed things radically. *(Hants Museums Service)*

Lavant Street looking down into the town, 1905. This busy Petersfield road was originally laid out as a direct approach to the station, when the railways arrived in the 1880s. The meadows it replaced had been known as Upper and Lower Drum Mead. Today, the names survive as part of a modern housing estate. *(Hants Museums Service)*

Chapel Street 1905. Chapel Street was developed in the second half of the 19th century as a major shopping area, following the arrival of the railways. Today, this aspect of its existence is little changed. *(Hants Museums Service)*

'HAMPSHIRE CHRONICLE,' Monday, June 2nd, 1777

"On Wednesday and Thursday last a cricket match was played on the Artillery Ground, London, for 500 1., the Hambledon Club against All England, which was won by the former. The particulars are as follows:

HAMBLEDON CLUB

	First Innings		Second Innings		Total
Brett	4.	c. Booker	1.	b. Lumpy	5
Small	5.	c. Lumpy	11.	b. Bullen	16
Francis	1.	b. Lumpy	0.	c. Booker	1
Sueter	12.	c. Booker	16.	b. Bullen	28
Aylward	10.	b. Booker	16.	b. Lumpy	26
					76

ENGLAND

	First Innings		Second Innings		Total
Bullen	0.	b. Brett	10.	c. Francis	10
Miller	29.	c. Sueter	8.	b. Brett	37
Lumpy	1.	b. Brett	0.	b. Brett	1
Booker	9.	c. Francis	2.	b. Brett	11
Braisier	1.	b. Brett	0.	run out	1
Bier	1.				1
					61
				Majority	15

This match was deemed the best ever played in London, the game having been at one time four to one against the Hampshire men."

St. Peter's Churchyard. Cricket lovers come here to visit the grave of the great Hambledonian, John Small and his illustrious family, the only stone now standing in the churchyard, near the entrance from the Square. The epitaph on his grave could be a precis of all such memorials:- "Praises on tombs are trifles vainly spent: A Man's good name is his own monument."

St. Peter's Churchyard, late 1940s. The churchyard was closed for burials in August, 1856. Apart from that of John Small, the gravestones were removed, and the graveyard levelled in 1950. *(Petersfield Society)*

Church Path. A haven of peace and tranquillity even today, just as Flora Twort depicted it in this simple pen sketch. *(Hants Museums Service)*

Dragon St. and Sun Inn *c.,* 1905. The old Sun Inn was originally built in the late 1600s. In 1976 it became The Green Dragon, taking its name from another famous inn, well known in coaching days, that originally was directly opposite. *(Hants Museums Service)*

St. Peters Road. This was once called New Way, and it was here stood Petersfield House, home of the Jolliffe family, one of the great 18th century families of the town. Sir William Jolliffe commissioned the William III statue, which originally stood here, prior to it being moved during the 19th century to its present site. *(Hants Museums Service)*

6. Village Hinterland

Lord Horder at Ashford. His Lordship was a great botanical connoisseur, and clearly he felt this particular specimen worthy of doffing his hat! *(Petersfield Society)*

Ashford Chace. The designs of Inigo Triggs set the scene for the loving care and development fostered on these gardens by Lord Horder for 40 years. *(Petersfield Society)*

50

Post Office, Sheet. The old bridge over the River Rother on the A3, taken either immediately before, or during the First World War. The new bridge was built during the early 1930s. *(Hants Museum Service)*

Sheet, St. Mary's Church and the Green. On the Green, surrounded by a protective fence, is the Chestnut tree planted to commemorate Queen Victoria's Diamond Jubilee in 1897. This photograph must have been taken shortly after the event. *(Hants Museums Service)*

Stoner, where the road goes down to Ashford. A scene still easily recognizable today, although the Petersfield/Alton road is far busier than in this pre-First World War picture. *(Hants Museums Service)*

Keepers Cottage, Stoner (demolished during the 1940s.) Thought to have been the cottage "Under storm's wing" in Edward Thomas's poem, "Interval":

"But the woodman's cott   It smokes aloft
By the ivied trees   Unwavering
Awakens not   It hunches soft
To light or breeze.   Under storm's wing."

Berryfield Cottage at Ashford, the first home in the area of the poet, Edward Thomas, although this photograph, taken in 1906, dates from before his time here.
(Bedales School)

Conversation piece in Church Road, Steep, about 1915. This rare photograph is a fascinating aside on English literary history. The lady holding the teapot is Mrs. Budd, of "The Cricketers" Public House. With her are Helen Thomas, wife of Edward Thomas and the Thomas's youngest daughter, Myfanwy. Another poet, Thomas Sturge Moore, lived in Church Road, Steep from 1922-32, in a house today marked by a plaque, and close to the Thomas's last home in the area. (Myfanwy Thomas)

Butser … The Road is the A3, during the 1890s, some three miles south of Petersfield, after the turning to Buriton. *(Hants Museum Service)*

At Buriton, 1890s. The Cottage was a pile of rubble by the turn of the century, although the garden survived for quite a time. *(Hants Museum Service)*

Buriton Church. This picture, and the previous print, are Frith studies, and were both taken at the same time. The ivy that clung to the tower is long gone, although the hooks that held it in place remain! *(Hants Museum Service)*

Otherwise the view is little changed, apart from the transport. *(Street)*

Westbury House. This fine mansion was the home of Colonel Le Roy Lewis. Situated eight miles from Petersfield on the West Meon Road, it was destroyed by fire on a November night in 1904. During the fire, the Colonel acted swiftly to save all but one of his family and staff, and the Portsmouth Evening News praised his "Sterling deeds of bravery, carried out with conspicuous coolness and courage." *(Standfield)*

East Meon Church, 1872. The earliest known photograph of All Saints church, East Meon, taken from Park Hill. The newly planted saplings in the picture were to grow into lime trees. *(Standfield)*

East Meon Fire, 1910. The fire came during a spell of hot and dry weather, on June 20th, due to an accident with a washing-copper fire, the village was suddenly threatened. A number of cottages were destroyed, and, in the words of the Petersfield newspaper, "The streets in the neighbourhood of the fire were piled up with furniture and the owners sitting in the midst sadly surveying the ruins of their homes." *(Standfield)*

High Street, East Meon. The date on this postcard is August 24th, 1908. An interesting period point is the break in the river fence, to allow cattle access to the water. *(Standfield)*

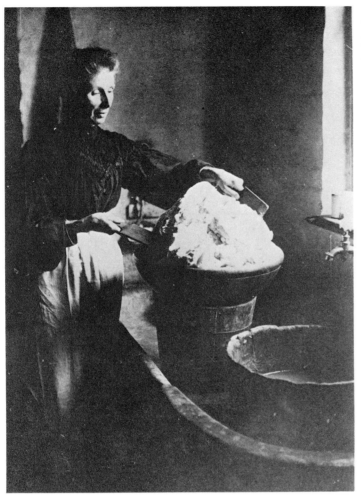

Making butter. Jane Wren of Riplington Farm making butter in the scullery in about 1908. The Wrens took over the tenancy of Riplington, between East and West Meon, in 1894. Isaac Wren held the post of Chairman of East Meon Parish Council from 1902, until his death in 1931. *(Standfield)*

West Meon in the early 1900s (below). A winter scene, with a leafless tree and snow melting on a porch roof. Judging by the stance of the man with the gun, and the position of the wagon and the small boy, this was clearly a posed picture. *(Hants Record Office)*

Leydene House. Formerly the home of Lord and Lady Peel, it was the scene of brilliant society parties. Lady Peel died in 1949, and the house was acquired by the Admiralty. Today, it is the wardroom of HMS Mercury. The Peels are buried at East Meon. *(HMS Mercury)*

The Plestor Oak, Liss. In this view, taken in about 1909, Plestor House is seen to the immediate left of the oak. It is mainly 18th century. To the far left is Henry Mells' grocery shop, and to the right, Miss Legg's confectioners shop. In these days, there was also a bank in one of these shops. On the extreme right of the picture is the Spread Eagle public house, dating from the eighteenth century. At one time, it was known simply as "The Eagle", and before that, "The Waggoners". *(Liss Area Historical Society)*

Liss School, about 1900. The school, which was built in 1870, is little changed today in appearance. Opposite the school, (known as the Board School in those days), behind the hedge to the left of the picture, is Forge House. It became a forge as its name implies after the building of The Board School, prior to which it was one of two Dame Schools in Liss, and was run by Mrs. Rhoda Budd. The other Dame School was in West Liss. *(Liss Area Historical Society)*

Lyss Place (Place House), Liss. This picture, taken from a painting reputed to be in the hands of the Coryton family, once of Lyss Place, then of Greatham Manor, shows the original house before it was pulled down in 1822. It had been the site of a Nuns retreat.

It was replaced by a Georgian House, which exists today. Only the refectory of the old building survived, and the new house was built onto this.

The Pond at Lyss Place, 1898. The pond has now been filled in, and no vestige of it remains today.
(Liss Area Historical Society)

Acknowledgements

Without the help and trust of many people both in guidance and in the loaning of photographs, this book simply would not have been possible. My gratitude goes to Mary Ray of the Petersfield Area Historical Society for pictures of the Girls' High School, and for checking factual material, David Scurfield of the Petersfield Society for his support, and the Society itself for many fine photographs, David Sykes, Librarian at Bedales School, for access to some fascinating school pictures, and the Headmaster and Staff at Churcher's College for allowing me to browse at length in their library. Also to Pat White of the Liss Area Historical Society for the photographs of bygone Liss, reproduced herein; I am grateful to Mr. F.G. Standfield, author of the excellent "History of East Meon", and to Stan Smith and Roger Hopkins for their expertise in reproducing some very rare photographs. My thanks to Alastair Penfold of the Hampshire Museums Service, and to Rosemary Dunhill, County Archivist and Miss S.J. Lewin, together with all the other helpful and painstaking staff at the Hampshire Record Office. Frank Westwood of the Petersfield Bookshop kindly permitted the reproduction of Hester Wagstaff's 1922 map of Petersfield. Invaluable help also came from Commander David Newberry of HMS Mercury, Mrs. Bridget Gledhill, a former pupil at Bedales, Mrs. Myfanwy Thomas, daughter of the poet, Edward Thomas, Mrs. Tania Barnsley, wife of the late Edward Barnsley, and Mrs. E.M. Larken of Buriton.

Hampshire Record Office.
Page 33   Top illustration. Ref: 198M85 B1
             Centre. Ref: 217M84/7
             Lower. Ref: 217M84/7
Page 56   Lower illustration. Ref: 200M85/5.

Select Bibliography

62

The History of Petersfield … Rev. J. Williams, 1857 (reprinted, The Petersfield Bookshop)

High Street, Petersfield … Petersfield Monographs No. 2. Petersfield Historical Society, 1984

Hampshire & the Isle of Wight … Brian Vesey-Fitzgerald. Robert Hale Ltd., London. 1949

Unknown Hampshire … Clive Holland. John Lane, London. 1926

Buriton & its People … E.M. Yates. Petersfield Papers No. 2. Petersfield Area Historical Society. 1976

Petersfield in Tudor Times … E.M. Yates. Petersfield Papers No. 5. Petersfield Area Historical Society. 1979

The Reputed Manor of Ashford … William Whiteman. Petersfield Papers No. 8. Petersfield Area Historical Society. 1987

Petersfield & Parliament … Nigel Surry. Petersfield Papers No. 7. Petersfield Area Historical Society. 1983

Petersfield under the Later Stuarts … James H. Thomas. Petersfield Papers No. 6. Petersfield Area Historical Society. 1980

Irregularly Bold, A Study of Bedales School … James L. Henderson. Andre Deutsch, London. 1978

The Petersfield Society Winter Newsletter, 1988

Domesday Book, Hampshire (History from the Sources Series) Ed. John Morris … Phillimore, Chichester. 1982

The Industrial Heritage of Hampshire & the Isle of Wight … Pam Moore. Phillimore, Chichester. 1988

A Walk in Winter … Sean Street. Enitharmon Press, Petersfield. 1989

THE HISTORY OF
PETERSFIELD

BY THE REV. J. WILLIAMS, M.A.

BEING THE SUBSTANCE OF A LECTURE DELIVERED IN THE NATIONAL SCHOOL ROOMS, MARCH 6TH, 1857.

THE ancient Borough of Petersfield stands on the very borders of Hants and Sussex, though situated within the former County: and its inhabitants, we think rightly, believe

The Neighbourhood

combines all that is beautiful in the inland scenery of both Counties. If we suppose the traveller approaching from the South, the scenery on his road over the wide spread Downs—while still the ruthless Enclosure Commissioner has work to do—will soon prove how properly the County has retained the appellation given to it by our Saxon forefathers, "GWENTSHIRE" or "open shire"; by a slight change, Hantshire; or more strictly if you will, South-Hantshire; the only trace now remaining of the several VENTÆ of antiquity.

In the numerous flocks that crop the thick and velvetty grass on the Downs, we can almost fancy reason good for a legislative enactment which forbade "any one farmer to keep more than 2,000 sheep, six score to the hundred":* while successive peeps into the valleys between, explain how easily the archers of the English army might have been supplied with bows of yew—that "Hampshire weed".

On the north of the Town again, another scene presents itself; and the traveller might fancy, though he has only passed some three or four miles, that an Electric shock had carried him at once to that

"land of brown heath and shaggy wood"

which the Poet would make us believe is peculiar to Caledonia.

The Parish of Petersfield itself, consisting of only 234 acres, presents almost every variety of soil that you could expect to meet with in a neighbourhood many miles in extent. Within an easy walk rare plants and ferns abound, to reward the Botanist. The Geologist can trace the commencement of the "*wealden denudation*" or the progress of the flint-stream amid the chalky ocean. Old vines on cottage walls bespeak another climate, where once was the haunt of the Beaver, and many an animal now unknown to the British Isles. Objects and scenes abound which may carry back in thought Geological and Botanical zeal to the mighty mammoths that roamed at large through the gigantic fauna of an almost tropical climate, in the pre-historic period.

But of these wonders other more scientific minds have promised to treat at no distant day. At present the History of Petersfield proper will supply us with an ample theme. Of the

Roman and Saxon

period little must be said: but we cannot refrain from noticing that the labours of the Enclosure Commissioner on our Heath, this last winter, has supplied an object for the exercise of Antiquarian lore. R. G. P. Minty Esq., our fellow-townsman, has sent this curiosity—an ovoidal pebble, measuring 8½ inches by 5½—to the learned Archæological Institute: and as they cannot decide whether it is a religious relic, or from the Sussex iron mines, or a real stone at all; who shall interfere?*

A Roman Camp is supposed to be traceable at Butser Hill, that highest point of the South Downs, 2½ miles distant from the Town, 916 feet above the level of the sea. And between Petersfield and Froxfield the remains of a Roman Villa and Camp have been discovered.*

This scanty notice must suffice for the earlier period of British or Roman story. And even of the Saxon period we have nothing to tell—rather humiliating to burgensian pride, when "Privett's flood" can tell of its humble herdsman who exacted vengeance on Sigebert, the royal murderer of the eolderman Cumbra.† Yet this is not extraordinary, when it is remembered that this neighbourhood was on the very borders of the vast wood of Anderida, that stretched over the en'ire extent of the Weald of Sussex—"112 miles or longer, from East to West, and 30 miles broad".‡ Petersfield must have seemed to the courtly Wintonian, at the very extremity of civilization.

We must begin our real and authentic history with the period of the

Domesday Book,

that great national record of England in the 11th century. There we read,—

"In Ceptune (*Finchdean*) Hundred the King holds Mapledresham in demesne. Ulvert held it. Queen Mathild (*wife of William I.*) owned it. In the time of King Edward (*the Confessor*) it was assessed at 20 hides (*circa* 2,000 *acres*): it is now 13. Here are 20 ploughlands (*as much arable land as could be managed with one plough and oxen in a year*). 4 ploughs are in demesne (*held for the proper use of the Lord of the Manor*). There are 34 villagers, and 15 borderers (*the latter a somewhat superior*

---

*25th Henry VIII, c. 18.

* Archæol. Jour. Dec. 1856.
* Arch. Jour. June 1855. † Ang. Sax. Chron. A.D. 755. ‡ Ib. A.D. 893.

grade to the former), who employ 15 ploughs. Here is a Church, and 8 servants, and 3 mills, which pay 20 shillings : and 5 acres of meadow. Here are woods which furnish 30 hogs for the pannage (*price paid for the run of a herd of swine to feed in the woods*). The herbage produces 6 shillings and 3 pence.

"Belonging to this manor Alboldus, the cook, holds 2 hides and a half. Tedgar held them in the time of King Edward, on condition that he should not remove elsewhere. This land was assessed above at half a hide, included in the other hides. There is 1 ploughland in demesne : and 5 villagers and 3 borderers with 1 plough : and 2 servants : and an acre of meadow.

"Belonging also to the abovementioned manor Tetbaldus holds 3 hides and a half. Richard de Tonebrige gave it to him when he had the land from the Queen. It is not now known on what title he holds. Two Rachemistre (*a class of Freedmen who served in war on horseback*) held them, and were not permitted to move elsewhere. There are 2 ploughlands in demesne : and 4 villagers and 8 borderers with 1 ploughland : and 2 servants : and 1 acre of meadow. A wood produces 6 pence.

"The whole manor, in the time of King Edward, was worth 25 pounds. It was and is now worth that sum. But those who hold it pay 32 pounds. Alboldus' share is worth 40 shillings. Tetbaldus' 4 pounds. "

But in the Domesday Book there is no mention of Petersfield by name. Mapledresham is synonymous with Maplederham,* and apparently the manor was co-extensive with the whole district of the united Parishes or Tythings. The Church at least is Buriton Church ; though the mills were probably, two in Sheet, and one near Petersfield.

Alboldus Cocus' land was most likely part of Nursted, since within the next century we find Geoffry Cook and his wife Eve, having fallen into the hands of the Jews, got free from their debt by means of the monks of Durford, to whom, in return for their hard cash, they gave lands at "NUTSTEDE".

Why the Saxons preferred Buriton to Petersfield, as a place of habitation, we need not wonder. If the opinion of Gilbert White,† as an advocate for Selborne's beauties, be true, surely Buriton Hanger may well compare with that of Selborne ; and the "Well-Head"—ere the Railroad embankment had hidden its beauties—might certainly claim precedence.

The population seems to have been 81 males ; which would give about 400 souls in all, as the inhabitants : while the value of the whole manor was 25 pounds. If this be compared with Eastmeon, that appears as worth 60 pounds, and there were 117 males, which would give a population of nearer 600 souls. The population of Hants in Domesday appears to have been 9,033—New Forest 217—Isle of Wight 1,124—Total 10,374.* There were 110 Churches, and 226 mills.

So that A. D. 1086, the period at which Domesday was completed, Petersfield *non est inventus*. However, we have some traces in our

Church,

that may guide us as to its date, and so we may gather the date of the town also.

Mr. Colson, our Winchester Architect, has, upon examination, decided that the West Tower presents traces of early Norman style, and is the earliest in the whole building : next in point of date is the North Door, with a window on the right, as you enter from the Square. The South Door is of a later date, and so also is the whole aisle on that side ; and it is not opposite the north door ; therefore we may suppose was not built at the same time ; in fact the Norman arches that remain are different in date on each side of the nave. But all round the outside may be seen the remains of Norman buttresses and mouldings ; and in the Churchwardens' store-room, the north wall of the Chancel still presents the remains of a Norman window. So that the whole Building seems to have been finished during the time of the Norman style of Architecture—the nave and north aisle first, and afterwards the south aisle.

If we now proceed to examine the

Interior of the Church,

we are at once struck by the Chancel Arch, which presents remains of the best period of the Norman style, yet not so *early* as the West and North Doors. Another look, and right and left, above the large arch, you see remains that suggest there was once a continuation of those smaller arches—In fact that was one side of a square tower, (as shewn in frontispiece) something like Eastmeon, St. Cross, and Winchester. And there is now an Inscription on the W. wall of the S. aisle, informing us that

" A wall eight foot long was taken down, and this pillar* and two arches new raised and turned. Also a wall of the same length taken down on the other side, and that arch new turned. Anno Domini 1731.
JOHN GAMAN & ARTHUR PESCOD, Churchwardens. "

These 8-ft. walls were the very supports of the old Tower, so that the four sides corresponded with the one now remaining. Look round at the capitals, and you will see some of early Norman style—earlier than that of St. Cross, which, according to Leland and Tanner, was built A. D. 1132. If you place yourself in the Nave and look at the east side of the Tower, you will see now the stone weathering, that tells where was the early Norman Roof. And if you wish to see some remains of that roof itself, you may see them in the timbers now serving as the roof of the south aisle, only lengthened to make them fit a wider space.

That South aisle seems to have been built, as already noticed, at a later period than the other parts of the building, with an Altar at the East end, and a Piscina, still remaining under the wainscotting in the South wall. Was it to serve in memoriam of some one of the Lords of the manor? Tradition speaks of it now as a "morning" (*sic*) chapel ; i. e. mourning—mortuary chapel.

As for the windows generally, they afford examples of style in—

Mapledersham, i. e. Maplederen-ham—village of the maple trees. *Saxonice.*
† Antiquities of Selborne, Letter II.
* Ellis's Introduction to Domesday.

* *Note.*—This Tablet was originally placed against the north side of the pillar in front of the reading desk.

East Window in South Aisle, circa A. D. 1300.
Another in the same aisle, near S. door, 1380.
East or Chancel Window, and the Font, 1400.
Windows in North Aisle with flat heads, 1500.

So that the building, as it exists at present, is a strange medley of styles and dates—not to mention the *Sash* windows, vulgarly called "Churchwardens'" windows.

Still we may fairly argue from the remains which exist, that the Church was begun soon after Domesday was finished, A.D. 1086; and perhaps by the same Architect that designed Eastmeon. And a Church of the same size as the present existed in Stephen's reign, or very shortly afterwards.

But who built Petersfield Church? There is an ancient Charter from William, Earl of Gloucester, giving the patronage of the Church of Mapledresham, with the Chapel of Petersfield, to the Nuns of Eaton (Nuneaton) in Warwickshire; reserving however, for his life, the rights and privileges to Thomas, who then held the Church. From the same Charter it appears that this Thomas was the grandson (*nepos*)* of Thurbratus, who held the Church at the time of the siege of Tolouse, A. D. 1159, 5th Hen. II; where Hamon, a brother of Earl William was killed. Now this would be as nearly as possible the date at which, to judge from the style, the South Aisle was built. Was the mortuary chapel then in remembrance of Robert, the father of William, or of his brother Hamon?

The West Tower and Nave, with perhaps the North Aisle, formed the Old Church; and this portion was no doubt built about A. D. 1100, if not earlier.—Perhaps by that great Church-builder, Matilda, the Lady of the manor, with the assistance of her cousin, Bishop Walkelin: just as most old parish Churches owe their foundation to the piety of the great landed Proprietors of the neighbourhood. But Petersfield quickly rising into importance, it became necessary to enlarge the Church; and additions and alterations were made, so that it appeared as in the frontispiece, A. D. 1150.

But who were these

Earls of Gloucester?

After William, the son of Henry I. had been drowned, a council of the Barons was held for the purpose of swearing fealty to Matilda and her infant son, as destined heir to the throne. Two chiefs then contended for the honor of precedence in this act of Vassalage. These were Stephen (nephew of Henry I.) and Robert, Earl of Gloucester, Henry's natural son. It is to be feared however, that no chivalrous feeling for an unprotected female led to this rivalry: for as soon as Henry died, Stephen seized the throne. And Robert seemed for a time well content in the quiet enjoyment of his manors and his property. But discontents arose; and Robert brought his sister Matilda over from France, and landed with her at Portsmouth, July 1138.

We need not detail the history of the many disastrous conflicts that followed, and made Hants,—and Winchester especially—the frequent scene of bloody strife. No doubt the men of Petersfield bore their part in the struggles conducted by their liege lord, Robert—a decidedly able man.

It seems that the manor of Mapledresham came to Robert from his royal father, who added this and the title of Earl of Gloucester, to make him acceptable to Mabell, the eldest daughter of Robert Fitzhamon, who died possessed of the Honor of Gloucester.

Robert of Gloucester, the historian, has preserved in curious rhymes, the courtship of Henry I., on behalf of his son Robert, with Mabell.

Earl Robert died A. D. 1147, and was succeeded by his son William, who married Hawyssa, daughter of Robert Bossu, Earl of Leicester, who founded the Abbey of Nuneaton in Stephen's reign: hence his gift to the Nuns of the patronage of our Church etc. It is worth while to notice the constitution of this Abbey—"for Nuns of the order of Fontevrauld; wherein, besides the Prioress and Nuns, there was for some time a Prior also, perhaps with men, as usually in the foreign houses of this order."*

This Earl William was the donor of the first Charter constituting Petersfield a

Market Town,

In the Parish Chest is preserved an old Charter to the following effect,—

" Know all men, present and to come, that I, Hawissa, Countess of Gloucester, have granted and confirmed to my Burgesses of Petersfeld who have built and are settled, and who shall build in it, all liberties and free customs in the same Borough which the citizens of Winchester have in their city, who are in a guild of merchants; and let them have the same (*liberties and customs*) in a guild of merchants as my husband, William, Earl of Gloucester, granted to them by his charter.

Witnesses:—William, Abbot of Dureford; William, Abbot of Chainsham;† Guido, Prior of Sandwich; Henry Hoese; William de Falaise; Robert de St. Remy; William of Suneward; Gregory, the Chaplain (*of Petersfield?*); &c."

The Charter of William is lost. But this is enough to make us see that Petersfield was a place of comparative importance in those days; not merely because it had the privilege of a *Market*, for a like privilege was bestowed on Selborne in the same century: but it had its Guild of *Merchants*, as Winchester, and a *Church* that would be suitable only for a goodly population. In the reign of Henry I. Winchester was in the zenith of its prosperity —of more importance than London. We are told indeed that a guild of Merchants was established there A. D. 856. It was the seat of Government in the time of Alfred. And in the time of the Roman occupation, there was a considerable woollen trade there; with an Officer to take such trade under his peculiar charge.* We can easily understand then that the tenants of Mapledresham manor, under the leading of a Lord of royal blood, would

---

* This rather militates against the Celibacy of the Clergy in that day.

* Tanner's Notitia Monastica.
† Chainsham Monastery was founded by the Earls of Gloucester.
* Camden. p. 118.

wish to take pattern from the courtly ways of Winchester. So that Petersfield—with all respect to its venerable mother, Buriton—having somewhat superior advantages of situation in its mills, its woollen manufactures, and its market, supported by the iron miners of Sussex, and the good monks of Durford, would soon outstrip its aged parent. So much indeed had it done so, that the infallible Pontiff! Alexander III. in his confirmation of Earl William's grant to Nuneaton, could only understand it to be "the *Church* of Petersfield with the *Chapel* of Mapledresham."†

But Earl William, his Countess, and their successors, were also considerable benefactors to Durford Abbey, which was founded by Henry Hoese of Harting, early in the 12th century. Successive landowners too, in Petersfield and Maplederham, contributed to propitiate the goodwill of the monks: no doubt it was well worth attention, if we may believe the pious canons themselves, who at Michaelmas, A. D. 1387, thus put down their spiritual advantages. Though, by what process such long exemption of days and years from the pains of purgatory was to be gained, they have not transmitted to us.

"Sum of the days of Indulgence at Buriton DCCC. IIII. XX. XV. (895,000 *days*), *summa dierum Indulgentie apud Buriton.*

"Sum of the years, MMCCCCLII years, 20 days."*

However, this interchange appears to have continued till the Dissolution, in Henry VIII., when Hethe House was held by a brother of the last Abbot, John Sympson.

When William, Earl of Gloucester, died, he left three daughters surviving him. After the Countess Hawisa's death, Henry II. married his son John, Earl of Moreton, to the youngest, Isabella (others call her Avisa, a name still remaining among the females of the neighbourhood, as "*Avis*"), and bestowed upon them the manors of the Earl of Gloucester. And there is a Charter from John still extant, similar in effect to that of his mother-in-law. After a while John grew tired of Avisa, and made excuse to the Pope that she was within the third degree of consanguinity, and so procured a divorce.

We are not told how John and his neighbours agreed while he lived at Eastmeon. But on his accession to the throne, he granted the manors of Maplederham and Petersfield to Earl Evreux, who had married another daughter of William, Earl of Gloucester. One would think it must have been rather a pleasure to have got rid of such a feudal Lord as John. Yet, short-lived must have been those feelings of pleasure, for Evreux and other Norman nobles soon gave John a pretext for seizing their English property.

But in A. D. 1215—the memorable year of Magna Charta—the manors of Petersfield and Maplederham were granted to Geoffrey de Mandeville, Earl of Essex, who had married Isabella, the *divorcée*. John however seems to have made a good bargain; for Geoffrey agreed to pay a fine of 20,000 marks for this and other property, while he (John) reserved Gloucester and Bristol for himself.

John never seems to have been able to continue long in friendship with any one : and so we find that Geoffrey soon forfeited his purchase. Amicia, third daughter of William, Earl of Gloucester, was now sole heiress of her father : she had married Richard de Clare, Earl of Hertford, and he received a grant of this property, and was thereupon created Earl of Gloucester.

In the reign of Henry III., 1262, this Earl Richard was succeeded by Gilbert Rufus, who at first took the side of de Montfort, but afterwards quarrelling with him, he joined the king's party ; commanding the 2nd brigade at the Battle of Evesham : where no doubt the men of Petersfield figured, as well as at the Battle of Lewes. In fact the Earl of Gloucester was second in point of power to de Montfort only, and it was his defection that mainly contributed to that nobleman's overthrow.

Men from Petersfield followed their royal Prince to the Crusades. For, besides the Earl of Gloucester, " Siward de Mapelderham " occurs among the names of those to whose property royal protection was given by Henry III. during their absence in the holy land.*

In the " Taxatio Ecclesiastica " 1291, 20th Edward I. Pope Nicholas granted the Tenths of all Benefices towards defraying the expenses incurred by Edward I. in his expedition to the holy land. It was made under the direction of John, Bishop of Winton, and Oliver, Bishop of Lincoln. There we find,—

	Taxation.	Tenths.
"Ecclesia de Mapelderham cum Capella	46*l.* 13*s.* 4*d.*	4*l.* 13*s.* 4*d.*
"Vicaria de Eastmeones	16*l.* 13*s.* 4*d.*	
"Prior de Seleburne apud Shete ad 17s.		
"Prior de Sancto Swithino habet maneria de Mapelderham 24*l.* 7s. 1¾*d* "		

Our connection with the Monastery dedicated to the memory of the " imbriferous " Saint of Winton, came about by an exchange, between the monks and Richard de Clare, of some land here for the Isle of Portland &c., A. D. 1272, 42nd Henry III. *Perhaps* that connection is the reason of Heath Fair being always rainy !*

That land was afterwards given to Magdalen College, Oxford, founded by Bishop Wainflect A. D. 1458, *temp.* Henry VI. We find in " Valor Ecclesiasticus ", Henry VIII. that this College had land in the parish, subject to a small payment to Petersfield Church.

That " War Tax " of tenths in Edward I. was succeeded in Edward III., 50 years after, by a war tax of ninths ; " *Nonarum Inquisitiones* ", meaning each to pay the same amount as in Edward I. This shews us that property had decreased one-tenth in value during that period of 50 years.

---

† Dugdale in Nuneaton.
* Blaauw's Dureford Abbey. p. 41.——Vespas. MSS. f. 84.

* Rymer's Fœdera.
* Swithin was buried in the open yard. The monks took it into their heads that it was disgraceful for so great a Saint to lie there, and so designed to move his remains into the Choir, July 15th. But it rained for 40 days after so heavily, they could not. *Brand's Pop. Ant.* 271.

There is no record of Petitions from Petersfield against this tax: they were all very well satisfied, even though it amounted to 2s. instead of our 1s. 4d. in the £. At least we may argue this, from the proceedings of the Rectors in those days. For we find, on reference to the old documents in Winton, that in the Episcopate of John, (al. Pontisera) Roger de Skeering, the Rector, had a license granted to him, of absence for the purpose of "*study*". In fact this laudable example seems to have been generally followed by succeeding Rectors. So that we may suppose they had not only the inclination to improve their minds, but also the means of carrying out their inclinations. Perhaps the war tax did not press so heavily on the people then; or rather we may say, human nature, the same then as now, felt some compensation under the burden of a war taxation, in the glory England gained: and in which no doubt many of the sons of Petersfield and Maplederham shared. Gilbert de Clare served in the Welch wars: he contributed as his part, ten Knight's Fees. He married Joan, a daughter of Edward I.*

At this period we have the first record of Members of Parliament for Petersfield. In a Certificate of the Sheriffs of England, of Knights, Citizens, and Burgesses, elected to attend the Parliament to be holden at Carlisle, 1307, 35th Edward I., we have,—

" Henricus de Celario
" Ricardus atte Brouke } pro burgo de Peteresfield. "

This honor had been *paid for* in the struggles that had been carried on temp. Hen. III. for Englishmen's rights and liberties, against a covenant-breaking King; and on the other hand, *earned* by the assistance given to that King and his son, as soon as those rights and liberties had been acknowledged and conceded. Petersfield and its liege lord played no mean part in those contests from which resulted the first English House of Commons. We therefore assert that the English Justinian (Ed. I.) only acknowledged a *well-earned* claim in summoning Burgesses from Petersfield to Parliament.

To Gilbert (the Red) succeeded his son Gilbert,* and he was a man of much importance and weight in the time of Edward II. Made Captain of the Vanguard of the army in Scotland, he was killed A. D. 1314, at the Battle of Bannockburn—that greatest victory that ever crowned the efforts of a Scotch army, and among the most fatal days to England—with more than the loss of Alma or of Inkerman, without the glory of victory.

Gilbert's only child married Hugh de Audelay, and their only child married Ralph, Earl of Stafford. This then became the influential family at Petersfield.

Observe, not *all* the land belonged to the nobles then. From the time of Domesday, others also held land here; and many Commoners were benefactors to Dureford Abbey in their own right. They had reason to be proud of their Dureford neighbours, who manfully upheld the British doctrine, against the pretensions of the Pope, " that no foreign prince, prelate, or potentate, ever had, hath, or ought to have any power or authority over this realm " in opposition or superior to our own laws.

Durford was favored (?) by a visit of Edward II. Sept. 8th, A. D. 1324, on his road from Petworth to Porchester. Did he pass through Petersfield and Langrish? or by Buriton, and so over the hills?

In Edward III. we find the Lord of Petersfield following his Sovereign to the French wars; holding an eminent command under the Black Prince at the ever famous battle of Cressy; and after the battle commissioned, with Sir Reginald Cobham, to report on the number slain; which they reckoned as 11 great Princes, 80 Bannerets, 1200 Knights, and 30,000 others. And also on the surrender of Calais shortly after, he was one of those appointed to take possession for Edward III. His son Hugh was also in the retinue of the Black Prince.

In an Inquisition, taken in 46th Edward III. 1373, the Borough was returned as worth yearly £6; a Market every Saturday worth 4s. yearly; two Fairs, on the feast of St. Peter and St. Andrew, (June 29, and Nov. 30) worth yearly 2s. 6d.; " also they say there are four Hamlets, viz. Maplederham, Weston, Nurstede, and Shete, worth yearly £9. also the pleas and perquisites of Courts there are worth yearly 20s."

In 1403, 4th Henry IV. Edmund, Earl of Stafford, was killed at the battle of Shrewsbury, fighting valiantly on the King's side.

What part Petersfield took in the religious struggles of those days, appears not—except that a brother of William of Wykeham was Rector of Maplederham, and it is not likely that he was merely a passive and silent witness of Wicliff's efforts.*

In Hen. V. and VI. the Earls of Stafford were prominent characters. In the latter reign they were made Dukes of Buckingham for their faithfulness to their Sovereign: taking part in the wars of the Roses, one of them was killed at St. Albans. Henry, Duke of Buckingham, was a principal agent in establishing Richard III. on the throne. " Troubled in conscience, (*so Dugdale*) that he had aided so murderous a usurper, " we soon find him giving his influence to the cause of Henry VII., then

---

* Among the records in the Tower of London, 24th Edward I. there is one of an enquiry, on the death of Gilbert de Clare, Earl of Gloucester and Hertford, as to his property &c. It appears from hence,—" Gilbert de Clare held the town of Petresfelde of his Lord the King in chief, as part of the honor of Gloucester : £7 15s. 5d. was paid yearly as rent by the freemen ; two Court Leets held yearly, 26s. 8d. ; a market 100s. per annum ; Pleas and perquisites of a Court Baron 26s. 8d. Sum £15 8s. 9d.

The same Gilbert had Maplederham manor, paying £10 7s. 10d. ; a water mill 10s. per ann. ; and other perquisites. Sum £13 20d. per ann."

* For an interval he was a Minor, and his mother married again Ralph de Monthermer, who held the property in that interval, and greatly distinguished himself in the Scotch wars.

* As Wykeham visited Selborne, (Vide White's Selborne, in loco.) it is likely that he paid his brother a visit at Maplederham Rectory, and probably made enquiries into the state of the parish.

In 1449, Waynflect (then Bp.) gave a benediction in the Church of the Monastery of St. Mary, Winton, to Mrs. Agnes Buriton, who had been elected and confirmed of that Society.

Earl of Richmond. He was unsuccessful: and seeking concealment in the house of a trusted follower, was by him betrayed. When he (Humphrey Banaster) claimed the reward of £1000, Richard III. answered, "He who would be untrue to so good a master, must be unfaithful to all others."

Again, his son Henry, through the knavery of a steward whom he had turned off for unjust practices, was attainted for treason in 13th Henry VIII., and lost his life on the scaffold.* Much of the property thus forfeited by the Buckingham family was restored to them. But Maplederham and Petersfield were granted, 20th Henry VIII. (1528), to Sir Henry Weston; from whom descended the Earls of Portland.

At this period a great change began through the whole kingdom. The Reformation affected civil as well as ecclesiastical matters. A new world was discovered by Columbus; and Trade and Commerce rose into proper importance. Freedom of religious thought and action soon was followed by civil freedom. Mark the order— First Gospel liberty; then other follows. Such is the history of all lands. And if you see for a time civil without religious freedom, it is only for a time. Civil power must yield to the tyranny of a few, unless religion enlighten the many: and, while enlightening, implant those principles which forbid our "using liberty for a cloke of maliciousness", or for any other object than the service of God our Saviour in the duties of our station, whatever that may be on earth.

In 6th Edward VI., A. D. 1552, Petersfield again sent

Members to Parliament,

Having omitted to do so from Edward I. It does not appear what causes led to the neglect of this privilege: perhaps the expense of paying* their Representatives for their services? Perhaps the satisfaction they felt under the protection of the powerful and good men that were Lords of Petersfield, made them also feel there was no need of other advocacy?

However, it is something to know that Petersfield had a share in the important measures of that Session in which was passed the Act for Uniformity of Service, according to the new Form of Common Prayer; and so establishing the Reformation in England. The Members appear to have been, Sir Anthony Brown, and John Vaughan, Esq. The Browns were a Surrey family of note in the two previous reigns; at this time possessors of Cowdray,† near Midhurst; afterwards created Viscounts Montacute, or Montague. The Vaughans were Hampshire people.

From that time Petersfield returned two members, until the Reform Bill—2nd William IV.—since which it has returned only one. The limits of the Borough were also extended by the same Reform Bill, so as to include the adjacent Parishes of Sheet, Buriton, Liss, Froxfield, part of Eastmeon, and Steep. And the right of voting, which, according to the Parliamentary Returns in 1831, was "in the Freeholders in general within the Borough" was extended to all £10 householders. The Returning Officer is now, as always, the Mayor.‡

The Reformation seems to have made good progress in Petersfield, if we may argue from a Roll of Popish Recusants, 34th Elizabeth, exhibiting only one name from Petersfield—"Thomas Neave, *nuper* de Petersfeld, Yoman"—and he appears to have left the neighbourhood. And even that name of "Neave" suggests suspicions as to its origin in Petersfield. For Bishop Gardiner, whose papistical tendencies are notorious, had given the right of presentation to the Rectory of Maplederham to one "Thomas Neave, Scrivener, of London, for this turn only." Surely enough to account for the recusants of "Buryton", as well as the one namesake at "Petersfeld". The same list gives the names of "Maria Ringe, wife of Rd. Ringe; Anthony Boyce, husbondman; Ursula Parson, spinster; all of Hambledon. Of Buryton, Thomas Kent, yoman; Johanna Crowcher; Arthur Rickman; Maria Blackman, wife of Henry Blackman; Emma Okelie; Elizabeth Geale; and Ralph Geale, yoman."

Sir Henry Weston sold his property to Thomas Hanbury, Auditor of the Exchequer, who died A. D. 1617. It appears that Hanbury and the people of Petersfield did not agree very well together, and there arose a long and costly lawsuit, as to whose were the market tolls &c. It was eventually decided in favor of the Hanburys. The whole Case is reported in a Book entitled "Report of the Case of the Borough of Petersfield:" printed by Thomas Davison, Whitefriars 1831. Several old documents are given there, of much interest: but its contents also suggest that there must have been something in the air of Petersfield of a sadly litigious element, in public matters especially: though no doubt it will disperse in *Petersfield future.*

There is a general idea that Petersfield was a place of very much more importance in the reign of Queen Elizabeth, than it ever has been since that period. Probably this idea arose from the above named Report. It is said that Queen Elizabeth gave Petersfield a Royal Charter. But no such document can be traced; neither indeed is a

---

* It seems to have been a peculiar misfortune of this family to suffer from the treachery of dependants. In 43rd Henry III. the then Earl and his brother had poison given them by his chief councillor, Walter de Scotney—the brother losing his life, and the Earl escaping only with a ruined constitution. It is to be hoped these wretches were not Petersfield men.

* 4s. a day for a Knight of the Shire. 2s. a day for a Burgess. 46 Ed. III. It is said that Andrew Marvel, M. P. for Hull, was the last that received this pay from a constituency.

† Edward VI. in a private letter to his favorite companion, Barnabe Fitzpatrike, (who as a boy had been appointed to undergo any whippings the royal Pupil might deserve) writes thus, Aug. 22, 1547,—
"We have been occupied in killing of wild bestes, in pleasant journeyes, in good fare, in viewing of fair countries; and came to Gilford, from thence to Petworth, and so to Coudray, a goodly house of Sir Antony Broune's where we were marvellously, yea rather excessively, banketted."

‡ Present Mayor, S. Seward, Esq. No. of voters on the Register, 331.

Royal Charter needed to constitute a Borough. Petersfield owes its privileges to a grant from its feudal Lord—just as Bristol did to the same Earls of Gloucester. But there is a Mace for the Mayor, with the Royal Arms on it, and the cypher E. R. with the date March 12, 1596.

In the above Report, the Mayor of Petersfield and others declare,—

> "The said boroughe heretofore hath maintained one thousand poore people in worke by the trade of Cloathing, without begginge, and hath maintained at publicke charge, besides everie man's private charge, forty men for the service of the Realme in the warres."

This latter fact may account for the Petersfield Coat of Arms : (*See Cover*) the Ring in the centre alluding to the chain armour formerly worn, and the four Pellets to the matchlock balls. But we must not suppose that all these "one thousand poore people" lived within the Borough of Petersfield, even if children were reckoned in with the men and women. For it is easy to prove that the population of Petersfield *never* exceeded that given in the 1851 Census, 1452 : besides 453 in Sheet. We may refer to our Parish Registers,* which begin A. D. 1558, the last year of Philip and Mary. It appears thence,—

36 was the average of Deaths for the next 10 years—Christenings, 25.8			
17.5	....	—	23
20	....	—	27.8
23	....	—	29.0

And this includes the year 1568, which reckoned 83 deaths in Aug. Sept. and Oct.—3, 4, 5, and 6 in a day, 140 in all. This plague appears to have originated among the soldiers withdrawn from the attempt to take Havre, as an equivalent for Calais.

Compare these figures with the Burials at the Church in the last 7 years, averaging 30 ; while those of the Nonconformists average 7 ; and the Baptisms 51.4, besides those of the Nonconformists. Could the population have been more then than now ?

Of the troublous times of the Stuarts, our space will allow us to say but little. Petersfield must have been the scene of frequent marchings and countermarchings, for other objects as well as to the battle of Alton and the siege of Arundel. The loyal Sir Edward Ford, of Uppark, no doubt had a wholesome influence on his neighbours. Few records remain, to tell us of the Religious state of Our Town in that day ; when the Clergy were ejected from 4,000 parishes, entailing sufferings on families reckoning 20, or 30,000 souls. Yet, no doubt, where all suffered in a measure, Petersfield was not exempt. An extract from the Register informs us,—

> "Memorand.—That Symon fflood, of Petersffeild, was Elected and Chosen Register for the said parish of Petersffeild, and sworn into the said Office the 7th day of December, 1653.
>
> Before us, THOS. COLE
> EDWD. HUGHES"

We fear there may have been a little of the Laudian leaven working then. At least our Parish Register gives some curious entries from 1632 to 1639, of "Licenses to eat flesh on days prohibited" signed "Ri. Antram, Curate." The names to which Licenses are, Stephen

Worlidge, gent. ; Mary and Barbara Yalden ; Mary, wife of Randoll Eames ; Arthur Bold ; &c.

The time came when men's eyes were opened to see the mockery of the fanatic legend on the Great Seal of England—"First year of Freedom by God's blessing restored 1648." (Liberty alas! then only a "cloke of maliciousness"!) But the Providence of God had brought good out of evil ; and we owe much to the period of the Commonwealth.

We must pass over lightly, as a doubtful *honor*, that Charles II. conferred on Louisa Querouaile the title of Baroness of Petersfield. It appears, from the Diary of Samuel Pepys, who was Secretary to the Admiralty in the reigns of Charles II. and James II., under date,—

> "May 1st, 1661. Up early, and baited at Petersfield, "in the Room which the King lay in lately, at his "being there. Here very merry, and played with our "wives at bowles."
>
> "3rd. Took Coach to Petersfield.........Here my wife "and I lay in the room the Queen lately lay, at her "going into France."

We cannot tell what other results then followed from the visit of the "merry Monarch"—a man that never kept faith willingly with friends or foes. How could he? since he was unfaithful to his own soul's best interests! Yet in after time it is said that there were those that lived at Heath House (Matthews), who often gave asylum to the fugitive Pretender ; while their friends the Carylls, of Lady Holt Park, forfeited all in support of the Stuart family. (*See Harting.*)

In the Diary of Mr. Samuel Pepys, Vol. III. p. 99, 4th April, 1667, we read,—

> "One at table told an odd passage of this late plague ; "that at Petersfield I think, he said, one side of the "Street had every house almost infected through the "town, and the other not one shut up."

We shrewdly suspect *the* Street will be at once recognized in Petersfield. In the Register of deaths for that year, A. D. 1666, occurs this entry,—

> "Thomas Trimmer, this was the first man that dyed of that most ffatall plague which happened in this towne the year above written ; he was buried April 5."

In June 1666 there were 64 burials, and 105 in July : total of burials that year, to Dec. from April 5th, 235.

Yet it is to this 17th century—so full of troubles on every side—that Petersfield mainly owes its Charitable Endowments.

1622 is the date of the Will of Thomas Antrobus, of Heath House, giving £100 "to build an Almshouse for poor lone men and lone women."

1664 John Goodyer, "for putting forth poor children of the Tything of Weston"—the overplus to be given to the poorest inhabitants.

1674 John Locke, of Sheet, "for teaching poor children of the said Tything to read the English tongue."

---

* Parish Registers were first ordered A. D. 1538, by Thomas Cromwell, Earl of Essex, as the King's Vicar General.

1690 Bishop Lanney, sometime Rector of Buriton, "for apprenticing poor children of Buriton and Petersfield alternately."

1722 Richard Churcher, of Petersfield, East India Merchant, gave £3000 "for establishing a College...... for boys to be taken out of, and belonging to the Borough of Petersfield........whose parents would give security to the Trustees, to oblige their sons to be bound apprentices to Masters of ships making their voyages to the East Indies."

In 18th Geo. II. "few of the inhabitants were inclined" or they "were not able" to have their children so apprenticed; and consequently it was enacted, that the Trustees should still apprentice "proper and qualified" boys as originally intended, and "the rest to such trades as the Trustees shall think proper and suitable." (*Report of Commissioners for enquiring concerning Charities.*)

At present there are 14 boys, boarded, educated, lodged, and chiefly clothed, until the age of 14 years; and a fee is paid on apprenticing them, from the funds of this Institution.

Besides the above, we have other Charities of later dates: viz.

1827 Miss Phillips gave the interest of £200, to keep certain tombs in repair, and the residue to the Officiating Minister and Churchwardens, to be laid out in Bread to be distributed "unto and among such poor men and women, resident in, and belonging to, the parish of Petersfield, who shall have attained the age of 52 years."

1828 Mr. John Meeres gave the interest of £166 13s. 4d. to keep certain tombs in repair, and the residue to be paid to the Curate or Officiating Minister of the parish of Petersfield, "to be by him applied in aid of the Sunday School of the said parish."

1846 Mr. John Lipscomb, wishing to imitate Mr. Meeres' good example, left a piece of land at Liss, intending the rent should be for the support of the National Schools, but the gift is pronounced void, under the Statute of mortmain.

1847 Mr. John Holland gave £5 a year, for Bread to be given to "such of the Poor of the parish of Petersfield as have attained the age of 55 years."

Our Parish Annals

Afford us some help in the history of our Town and Parish. The entries at the beginning of the last century bespeak a state of things not favorable to religious influence. The Parish Vestry was generally (if not always) after Divine Service on Sunday. (Yet this was ordered by Act of Parliament, 43rd Elizabeth! Far be such Acts from the Parliaments of our day.) So that we are prepared for such a record of utter selfishness as the following in 1741. "Prosecution agreed to against Buriton Parish, for bringing in a Dung Cart, a sick Vagrant woman and setting her down by the road-side, where she shortly after dyed, and so became a charge to this Parish."

The sin, observe, being the charge and expense.

In 1727, it appears a scheme for building a Workhouse was set on foot.* The Poor and the Workhouse regulations seem to be the chief topics; and the entries display a sad state of immorality: one of the least gross of the vices being gin drinking and drunkenness *in* the Workhouse.

In 1743, the weekly cost of Pauper maintenance was, for each child 1s. 9d., and for the rest 2s. per head. In 1752 1s. 8d. and in 1766 1s. 9d. per head was allowed. In each case the Contractor made what he could of the Pauper's labor. This seems a much cheaper scale than at present. Provisions, no doubt, were cheaper—as indeed appears from the following prices, taken from the Overseers' accounts in 1735—Beef 2½d. per lb.; Mutton 3d.; Lamb 3d.; Veal 2½d.; Cheese 3d.; Butter 5d.; Sugar 5d.; Soap 4½d.; Candles 5½d.; Bread and Flour 10d. to 1s. per gallon; Oatmeal 10d.; Salt 8d.†

It is not easy to ascertain the true cost of maintenance of the Poor in those days. In 1764, the Poor-Rate appears to have been about £300 for Petersfield. But then the Church-Rate was in great measure also expended on the Poor. "People with Passes" were a great tax. In 1757, 265 such were relieved in *one month*, at an expense of £7 7s. 6d. Then the Churchwardens' accounts exhibit continual entries for slaughter of "varmint" of all kinds —sparrows and polecats—hedgehogs and foxes and martins. How a parish of so small an acreage came to abound in such like "varmint", does not appear! Cunning hunters must have abounded within its precincts.

However, we can easily understand that, in this way the Rates were in 1749 considered "so burdensome the people were scarce able to bear them": in 1754, there appears by the rate-book to have been 20 empty houses: and in 1758, an Order in Vestry "ordered the wearing of Badges (Will. III. 8 and 9) to be strictly enforced on all receiving relief".

All this has passed away. The Poor are no longer classed with the "varmint"; and Petersfield is now the centre of a "Union" of 13 Parishes, and a population of **7814**. And while our Union House can insist on strict morality within its walls, it can also shew rosy and cheerful faces, such as the old system never could.*

Nevertheless, there was a spirit of improvement at work in those days. In 1731, the Churchwardens had effected what they considered a great improvement; (*See* p. 8) other people may think differently. In 1754, the Steps, Wall, and Gate were erected on the East side of the Churchyard, "opposite New Street"

---

* Not finished till 1746.

† In Henry III. and Edward I. the ordinary price of a quarter of corn was 4s.—a sheep 1s. So meat was cheaper and corn dearer (relatively) then, and 120 years ago, than they are now.
6d. an acre was the average price of land in the 13th century.

* In 1801, the Population of *Petersfield* was 1159; the Rates, at 6s. in the £, were £418 5s. 5d.
The Population of *Sheet* at the same date was 247; and the Rates, at 2s. in the £, were £151 3s. 6d.

1759, " Windows in Church were mended ".

1760, " Paid for a Peck of Rye for Paste for ye Commandm^ts. 2s. 0d." (was this to restore the Chancel &c. ?)

1760, " Leave was given to erect a Gallery on the North side, by Subscription. " And " the Church was Whitewashed. "

1765, Repairs, to some extent, were again executed in the Church. There occur also sundry payments for " Bass Viol strings "—for the parish was attentive to the Church Music.

From 1750, the Bells appear to have been under consideration, and sent for re-casting; and in 1770, this matter seems to have been finally arranged, under the advice of " Mr. Pack ".

About this period occur various entries of money paid to " *Wm. Batt* "; until in 1758 it stands, " Pd. Wm. Batt, *for looking after the Clock*, £2 0s. 0d. " There is no entry of what the Clock cost; as in the Buriton accounts. The Town Engines make frequent items in the expenses.

The zeal of the Churchwardens seems to have been very exuberant. One is ready to fear that much of their valuable time must have been spent in hunting up disorderly characters on the Sunday. However, they seem to have had their " expenses on walking on Sundays " paid to them; as no doubt they deserved: especially if the entry, " Visiting Public Houses in time of Divine Service, 1s. 3d. " mean that they were obliged to taste each Tap they visited on their Walk. What rate-payer then could hesitate to allow, as appears in 1773,—

" Paid new Churchwardens, balance, £1 11s. 4¾d.

Expenses [!] at same time .... 3s. 4d. "

The Visitation trip was .... " £1 18s. 0d.

The Rev. Jno. Street, Curate, his expenses 0 8 0 "

But Office then was a high distinction. Indeed as early as 1698, an entry occurs of the old Overseers appearing before the Magistrates, and handing over to the three new Overseers " three gold rings of 7 d. weight, valued at £1 18s. " (? emblems of Office) as well as the balance from the Rate. This ceremony of institution continued for many years. But how those rings disappeared no record remains.

Petersfield felt an interest also in the world without. Besides the usual loyal demonstrations, we find,—

In 1756, " Paid Ringers when Governor   s.   d.
          Blakeney went through 3   0 "
1758, Aug. " Pd. Ringers on account of
          taking of Louisburg......... 9   0 "
  ,,   Sept. " On account of King of Prussia's
          victory 6   0 "
1761, " On acct. of King of Prussia's victory 10   0 "

This martial ardour seems to have been especially encouraged by the fact of " a Camp on the Heath " in 1758, and on account of a Guard-room there, the Parish paid £4 6s. 0d. In 1768, Robberies were so frequent, that a Vestry was summoned to devise means for checking

them. So that martial discipline was not omnipotent.

Then followed stirring times of war. In 1796, a Rate of 6d. in the £ was levied, for providing Seamen, and paid over to Government.

Yet, in 1793 a Militia Substitute cost £35 13s. This must have been from scarcity of men, not lack of ardour. Again in 1798, " April 13th, The inhabitants of Petersfield paid into the Bank of England £88 10s., as their Voluntary contribution for the Defence of the Country."

Everybody then was a warrior. Aunts could write to their nephews,—" I should be glad to see you for a few days, if you could make it convenient. But as you are turned soldier, and I hope in a right cause, I do not desire it till the war is over. *I love you the more for your love of your King and Country.* " The foregoing is from a letter written by an old dependant of the Gibbon family to her nephew, Mr. R. Jouning, of Petersfield, one of the " Armed Association " Corps. This Corps found their own Uniform, and Government supplied the Arms. £65 8s. 6d. was collected for instruments for the Band. This Subscription was made up by the names of
Bonham, Patrick, Baker, Mundy, Ring, Whicher, Andrews, Lear, Matthews, Redman, Meeres, Child, Watts, Powell, Padwick, Dusautoy, Bayton, Johnstone.
It was a time of enthusiasm. The prisoners of war made " Frenchman's Lane " then a reality.

It is curious to notice how many names of olden time still remain. A hundred and sixty years ago, the Petersfield Rate Book gives, in order following, the names of
Gamon, Woolridge, Allin, Robinson, Colbrook, Young, Eames, Knight, Baker, Thorpe, Hudson, Tribe, Westbrook, Walker, Bradley, Parker, Powell, Mills, Henty, James, Restall, Winter, Goldringe, Meeres, Pearse, Brown, Bridger, Lipscomb, Adams, Todman, Chitty, Cheas, Pocock, Munday, Rickman, Pescod.

The first entries of " *Christenings* " A. D. 1558, give the names of Hall, Hart, Preston, Marsham, Bristow, Fawkner, Wycher. Of " *Burialls* ", Almye, Osburne, Baily, Baker, Johnson, Swallow, Goldringe. Of " *Marriadges* ", Richard Hall and Mary Randall, Richard Cooper and Margaret Neale, John Crowcher and Joane Hall, William Bould and Mary Heath.

If we thus see how far the names of the inhabitants have changed, let us also see what other

Changes have taken place.

Fifty years ago, Petersfield had no such Room as our National Schools now afford. There were schools indeed of some repute for the upper classes—the Misses Parr and Wheatley, Messrs. Wells, Dusautoy, and Trodd. And the Library and Reading Room, established 1838. But the education of the Poor was far behind, in spite of Goodyer and Locke. In 1748, the Vestry resolved in solemn conclave, " to allow Mrs. Worledge one shilling pr. week till her school increased. " What sort of a School such a Mistress kept may be easily guessed. The following curious entries in the Overseers' accounts tell of scholastic progress :

1698.—" Paid Mr. Mayr. for spinning wheels and what belongs; and for learning the poor to spin, 5*l.* 7*s.* 0*d.* "

1741, Aug. 3.—" Spent at the beakers Arms, upon the piepell that was at the festre miting, 0*l*. 2*s*. 0*d*. "

Aug. 13.—" Paid for a hors to porch rnouth to sine ye rate, 0 2 0 "

Nov. 3.—" Paid to a chimney swiper for swipen of the chimney at the W- .khouse, 00*l*. 0*s*. 4*d*. "

1750. Feb.—" Paid H. Wells for bleeding Dame Miller, 0 0 4 "

Fifty years ago, Mrs. Brown, in High Street, had her school for petty tradespeople. Then one Mrs. Lock went to Winchester to learn the system ; and afterwards kept a school on "the Bell system,"(?) in the vestry. Mr. Cobden, who had a flax factory, at the Spinning House, on the Winchester road, put some of his workpeople's children to school, to learn *reading and knitting*. Nor must we omit the first Night School, kept by Mr. Wetherspoon. Then there was a school in the time of Rev J. P. Maurice, in the old Chapel at Heath House. And at last, in 1837, the Schools in Golden Ball Street were built, for 160 children, allowing two-thirds the space now felt to be required for each child—a work far in advance of the average attainments of that day. In truth we must ever acknowledge a deep debt of gratitude to the Pioneers in moral and spiritual progress of the last 50 years. It is well for us who are now, that they came before us.

When a Savings Bank was introduced in 1842. all seemed satisfied. No one then dared even to dream of the progress made in our day. No doubt it was considered a daring plan to add a British School in 1845, for 110 children. But when, at Christmas 1853, new National Schools were spoken of ; many, we fancy, treated the scheme at first as a hoax. Yet the liberality of friends gave a ready response. At a cost of £1809 17s., in six months our fellow-townsmen, Messrs. Minchin and Wetherspoon, accomplished Mr Colson's design ; and on Nov. 28th, 1854, the Schools were opened by the Bishop of the Diocese ; and now reckon upwards of 300 children, under the care of nine trained Teachers, competent to teach not only "reading and knitting", but all that is needed for a sound Commercial education ; at a rate of payment within reach of the poorest. We only congratulate ourselves that we have no disciples of Malthus to deal with : for we suspect our new Schools have much to do with the health of our juvenile population ; since the average of Deaths among the scholars is 1 per cent., against 2 per cent. of the rest of the parish—the reverse being the usual case.

The New Schools have been the means, with the aid of Sir W. G. Hylton Jolliffe, of restoring an old Street. THE MINT we fear is of modern date, and inglorious origin in a garden there, noted for a herb which supplied a quondam panacea—"Mint Tea". Yet there is something in the idea of a *money-mint*, as connected with Petersfield. For Akerman notes, as a scarce coin, a penny of Robert Earl of Gloucester. Mr. Jouning has Tokens of "Thomas Jaques, at the White Harte, in Petersfield" date probably 1660 ; of "John Jones" ; and of "Holland and Andrews" in the last century. Where these were coined appears not. But what is now HYLTON ROAD was a Street 150 years ago, with small houses on each side, and by the little stream were tan-pits. These houses were pulled down to make the grounds for the House that Mr. John Jolliffe built in the Lawn, where was previously the residence of Mr. Mitchell, whose daughter and heiress he married. That House stood little more than 60 years, ere parish disputes led to its demolition.

There was a shop or two by the Churchyard steps also pulled down. The New Way was then opened ; and King William sat on a *Golden* Horse, opposite the entrance to Mr Jolliffe's, in the New Way. The *Golden* Horse was moved to its present site, in the middle of the Square, about 50 years ago, and was then *painted*. Here stood the ancient Market House, with its Court Room and Black Hole ; the door of the latter still doing duty at the Town Hall, built by Col. Jolliffe, in 1824.

Sundry flat stones about the open Square mark where the ancient shambles stood. The residence of J. Bonham Carter, Esq. was once the Castle Inn, where Charles II. and his Queen-mother slept, *en route* to France—where the " merry monarch " played at bowls ; as Mr. Samuel Pepys did, and has duly recorded it in his Diary.

On the pedestal of the once *golden* but now *painted* Horse is the following Inscription,—

> Illustrissimo Celsissimo Principi
> **GULIELMO TERTIO**
> Qui ob plurima quam maxuma Officia
> De his Gentibus optime meritus est
> Qui Rempublicam pene labefactam
> Fortiter sustentavit
> Qui purum et sincerum Dei cultum
> Tempestive conservavit
> Qui legibus vim suam Senatuiq : auctoritatem
> Restituit et stabilivit
> Gulielmus Jolliffe Eques
> Ne aliquid qualecunque deesset Testimonium
> Quanto cum amore Studioq : tam ipsam Libertatem
> Quam egregium hunc Libertatis Vindicem
> Prosecutus est
> Hanc Statuam TESTAMENTO suo dicavit
> Et in hoc Municipio poni curavit

Exts. { Samuele Tufnel
Edvardo Northey
Johanne Jolliffe

SHEEP STREET, with its "Shoulder of Mutton and Cauliflower" sign, once deserved its name as the Sheep-Market. Whether " THE SPAIN " was so called as the Market for Spanish wool, does not appear. But the Horse Market was held there till lately, when the weekly Market of Saturday was changed to the fortnightly Wednesday—a downward change ! yet on a par with the case of Episcopal Chichester. However, the old Fairs survive, on the days of St. Peter and St. Andrew (old style) ; and a new Fair is added on Oct. 6th. Who can tell what the Rail may add ? If the twenty-seven Coaches that, 25 years ago, passed through Petersfield daily—besides Vans and Road Waggons—could not retain a second M. P. for the Borough, *they* have only one representative now, in our Royal Day Mail, driven by that well known Artist of the aristocratic " Rocket " ;* while its proprietor, " Mine

---

* Mr. F. Faulkner has occupied " the Box " for above half a century.

Host" of the *Red Lion*, still survives; although his Brethren have passed away from the *Old White Harte*, in High Street, (where Magistrates sat in Petty Sessions), with its *Folly*, leading into College Street. The *Green Dragon* has given way to the *Sun*, and like the *Golden Ball*, survives only in the name of the Street in which it was situated. HIGH STREET is HIGH STREET still. PARSONAGE STREET, having lost its Ministerial Dwelling within the last hundred years—though after that honored for a while with the Poor House—has hidden its shame in the BACK LANE. The WINCHESTER ROAD—formerly STONHAM STREET—for a time had the name of CHAPEL STREET, in memory of the pious efforts of the Rev. R. Denshaw; the scene of whose labors was first in that Street, though they terminated in the Chapel in COLLEGE STREET, built by his means, in 1801; the Galleries were added in Mr. Greenwood's time—men whose labors of love may well lead the historian to "rejoice in Christ preached sincerely, not of envy and strife," by them. The Chapel now stands on the site of the Old Poor House. The College was built in 1729. Between that and the Yew Hedge that marks the "Tor Plot" at the foot of RAMSHILL, was the Marsh; a noted winter resort of wild fowl. But how long will the name of RAMSHILL continue? Will it be "THE HILL OF SLEEP" after the CEMETERY is finished?—a work at which we scarce know whether to sorrow or rejoice. Rejoice we must, that St. Cuthbert's† influence no longer avails, to heap masses of corruption where the living resort. Yet sorrow we must, that touching associations should be taken away from our houses of prayer; and that our hallowed meetings should no longer be solemnized by the sight of affection's tribute, in the Sculptor's* art, or monumental record. Still we must own the beauty of the situation, and its retirement, claim some measure of admiration; and the design of the Mortuary Chapels cannot fail to add to the high character of the Architect, as well as to the attraction of the place.

Even the "Ruthless Enclosure Commissioner" has added to our improvements nearly 50 acres of "Recreation Ground" on the Heath. Perchance we may see the "Cranberry Garden near Hethe House" restored, as in olden time? The newly established Horticultural† Society should see to this. Who can tell what is not in store for Petersfield future? When the Railroad is completed, and "*Station Street*" has its houses occupied; when other *Streets* and *Crescents* and *Squares* demand an enlarged supply of Gas‡—those who live to see that day may describe it. The days of flax,§ woollen,‖ and fringe¶ factories may have passed away for ever: as well as the "healthful odour of the tanyards" (!!). But the fresh and bracing air of our SOUTH DOWNS, none can take away. The Rails are laid, and our Engines are running on the line, for the moral and spiritual improvement of the people. Our monthly County Court, and fortnightly Petty Sessions, administer the law of the land. Our District Visiting and Maternal Societies, and Clothing Club, seek to "fulfil the law of Christ".

Some speak of "good old times" in the past. The records of Petersfield, however, do not forbid the hope of *better* times coming. Only let each one do the work God has given each to do in their day. Let our "Philharmonic" and "Improvement" Societies be emblematic of the future rivalry in "love and good works." Let the name of "PETERS-FIELD" remind us of the true basis of all real progress; the Gospel of Grace; the ROCK on which to rest while the world is moved. "Both young men and maidens; old men and children: Let them praise the name of the Lord: for his name alone is excellent: his glory above the earth and heaven. Ps. CXLVIII. 12, 13.

THE NEIGHBOURHOOD.

In a sketch of the Neighbourhood, we must first notice our venerable Parent,

BURITON.

It has been already stated that a Church is mentioned in Domesday. But the present structure contains no remains of earlier date than Petersfield. The Norman arches record the Church-building spirit that prevailed in the 11th and 12th centuries. The "Aumbrye" or locker, and "Sedilia", and general style of the Chancel, bespeak a later period. The picturesque and ivy-covered Tower has its history preserved in the Church Book:—

"Memord.—Munday morning, between 4 & 5 of the "Clock, the 17th day of November, Anno 1712, Berri"ton Steeple, being shingled, and about : 80 : foot high, "took fire, by a very Terrible Tempest of Thunder and "Lightning, nigh the top, and was Burn'd down: the "foure Bells were brak down and melted. And the new "Tower was Rebuilt in Anno 1714. And the 5 new Bells "were hanged up Anno 1715, at the expense of the Pa"ish, and by severall good Benefactors. The Barnes at "the Manor house oft times caught fire, but the People "prevented the damage, and saved them."

The Clock too, goes back to the same date, nearly:—.
"April 19ye, 1720, Agreed then wy. Mr. David Com"pigné, Clockmaker, to keepe the Church Clock at Ber"riton in good Repaire for twenty years to come, at five "shillings yearly, if he shall live so long, all casualties "excepted, the Parish finding Clock lines.

David Compigné."

---

†Cuthbert died A. D. 758. It is said that by his influence was introduced the custom of interment in Towns, rather than in the suburbs.

*There is a work from Chantry's chisel in the Chancel, to the memory of one of the Blunt family—old residents in the parish.

†The first exhibition of this Society took place in 1856.

‡Gas was first introduced into Petersfield in 1852.

§Flax was grown in Petersfield 50 years ago.

‖Shoell's (a Devizes man) where White, the Basket Maker, is now.

¶Buxton's, where Nichols, the Chemist, is now.

And from the same Book we learn the cost of the Tower to have been " £320 15s. 07d "; and of the Clock " £20 00s. 00d ".

The mural monuments in the Church tell us of the various landed proprietors of the parish. The families of Hanbury, Bilson, **Holt**, Hugonin, Lee, Hely, Haw, Askew, King, and various Rectors. One name is not there; and that of some note—the name of Gibbon, the historian. His family acquired property in Buriton and Petersfield early in the 18th century. The present Manor House was chiefly built by Gibbon's Father: who, as a " South Sea " Director, became involved in the general ruin that fell on that Company. The family, however, re-purchased the Buriton property. The elder Gibbon was some time M. P. for Petersfield in 1734; and Gibbon himself was a Candidate for the honor; as appears in the following Speech, delivered by him on the day of Election for the Borough of Petersfield, in the year 1761.

" GENTLEMEN,

I appear here in a situation very different from my expectations. I hoped to have stood here, the assertor of our common Independency. I can only lament, with you, a yoke it is impossible to shake off.

The most considerable part of the still remaining Independent Freeholders of this Borough, addressed themselves, some time ago, to my Father, as a Gentleman whose past conduct had deserved their esteem, and desired he would offer himself as a Candidate.

They were justly provoked at so many Nominations, with the mockery of Elections where gentlemen were returned for the Borough, who hardly knew in what County it was situated. My Father accepted their offer with thanks; but soon afterwards (I fear out of an ill-grounded partiality) desired they would transfer the honor of their choice upon me. I had the satisfaction of receiving that mark of their approbation.

From that time I had the greatest reason to hope for success. Without threats; without promises; by no methods I should blush to acknowledge in this place; I could without presumption promise myself the majority of the real Independent Freeholders; in opposition to that unknown Candidate, with whose name we are but just made acquainted.

One man disappointed all these hopes; a man who, after every engagement which could bind a Gentleman or an honest man, infamously abandoned me.

This treachery, and the consequences it hath had, leaves me nothing else to do, than to express my most grateful sense of my obligations to my friends—obligations unconnected with success; and which, were every nobler principle wanting, my pride would never suffer me to forget.

Had I succeeded, I should have used my utmost endeavours to have acted up to the great trust reposed in me. I should have considered a seat in Parliament neither as a title of honor, nor as an instrument of profit, but as a laborious and important duty; to which the greatest Parts, joined to the severest application, are scarcely equal. I should have endeavoured to follow the path of moderation and impartiality: loyal to my King, without servility; zealous for my Country, without faction; attached to the general welfare of Great Britain, but not inattentive to the particular interests of the Borough I had the honor to represent.

Excluded from this agreeable prospect, I must confine my ambition within the duties of a private life: and I hope my behaviour, as a man, and a neighbouring gentleman, will never make my friends repent their having thought me worthy of a higher character. " *

J. Bonham Carter, Esq. M. P. is now the proprietor of the Buriton Estate; and the Rev. W. Legge of the Weston. Buriton has a National School for Girls and Infants, built in 1844. The Primitive Methodists have a small Chapel, which stands back from the Village High Street, as seeming to court retirement.

Of the rest of the Parish we must add little, save that an annual Rent-charge from the Nursted Estate, paid to Corhampton, still keeps up the remembrance of the old connexion with their common Lord, the Earl of Gloucester. And it appears as if the present division of " MAPLEDRESHAM " into the several Tythings of Maplederham proper, Wes*ton*, (or West Maplederham) Nurstede, Petersfield, and Shete, dates from the 12th century.

Travelling with the Sun, we pass from Buriton to

LANGRISH,

(a Hamlet of Eastmeon) where is the Residence of J. H. Waddington Esq. a branch of an old Surrey family. Although the present House was built by its present occupier, our Parish Chest tells of one " Robert Le Vowell, " of Langrissche, and Alicia his wife, who gave the bur- " gesses of Petersfield an annual rent of twelvepence, " from a tenement in Stonham Street, Petersfield, held " by Nicolas Colebrok. " Anno 46 Edwd. III. (1273).— a Charity now lost.

EASTMEON

has several points of interest. We first come to its nice Schools, built in 1844, for 250 children. The Manor was given by Bishop Alwyn to Winchester Cathedral. And the present Church—a fine specimen of Norman Architecture— was built by Walkelin, (Bp. of Winton) a cousin of William I. It was originally a cruciform structure, with the Tower at the intersection. A South Aisle was added about A. D. 1280: with many details, of various later dates still. The Spire is also a later addition; the Bells, if any, in that day must have been placed in another tower. For it is quite plain that the present Tower was open all the way to the top. The Font appears to have been carved by the same hand, and cut from the same material as that of Winchester Cathedral; repre-

---

* We are indebted to Sir W. G. H. Jolliffe for the copy.

senting, in order, the Creation of Adam; the formation of Eve from the rib of Adam; the temptation; the expulsion; and the instruction of Adam and his wife in the arts of husbandry and spinning. The Pulpit is of stone, but of late date. There is a relic of the Middle Ages, in the "Saints' Bell", hung in one of the windows of the Tower. And no doubt there are many other interesting remains hidden beneath the accumulation of plaster and whitewash. The Pews and Galleries are most unsightly, and in a deplorable condition; while the walls and ceiling are disfigured by hideous daubs of color. Sad indeed is it that we must record that the attempts of the Vicar and other friends, have failed to effect a Restoration.

Directly opposite the Church, is an old house, often called "King John's House". Yet the present structure is not of so old style. Though there still exists a Refectory of ample size; and other remains that betoken a large mansion. And it is evident from Domesday Book, that it was an important locality then; if not also in the time of the Romans.

At any rate, remains of a Roman Villa* are traceable at

FROXFIELD.

This is a Chapelry of Eastmeon; and the Church exhibits some specimens of Norman style. There is a School, endowed by the liberality of R. Love, Esq., of Basing, (1721); and F. Beckford, Esq., (1767): and Basing still supplies, in the name of Martineau, munificent contributors to the cause of education and Christian Charity.

Passing along the ridge, we come to Views which are scarcely to be surpassed—whether we allude to the extent of that from Old Stonor Hill, or to the more limited and picturesque scene along the New Road. At least we can say that the latter—situated within the Tything of Ashford, in the Parish of

STEEP—

runs through a Manor, perfectly unique in its customs.

Ashford Manor

dates from 11 Henry VI. (1453). The Tenants holding land, were their own Lords; though acknowledging the paramountship of Eastmeon. Upon admission at Eastmeon Court, they became tenants of Ashford, paying 12d. as a Heriot; which, with other fines, they divided among themselves; appointing their own manorial Officers.

This Parish, like Froxfield, is attached to Eastmeon. There is a nice School Room, close to the Church.

Steep affords a curious example of the origin of Parishes, as commensurate with the Estate of the Founder of the Church; having attached to it, the Tything of Ambersham—a strip of land, 9 or 10 miles long, and about 12 miles distant, in the neighbourhood of Midhurst.

* Archæol. Jour. June 1855. p. 199.

LISS

is a Parish of ancient date. It appears from the Domesday Book, that most of the land then belonged to the Abbess of Winchester. LISS PLACE evidently was a Religious Establishment, and can still shew a large Refectory. Here is a miserable example of mis-appropriation of Church property—the income of the Incumbent being £96 per annum, and no house; with a population of 748, scattered over 3679 acres.

There are two Endowments for Schools, of £4 and £3; the gift of the Cole family.

EMPSHOTT,

the adjoining Parish to Liss and Greatham, has a very singular Church, with early Norman remains. In the narrowness of its aisles, it is unique; and the rood screen is of a beautiful design. The residence of Mr. Cobden is generally supposed to have been built by one of the Regicides; or more likely by the Captain of the Guard at the Execution of Charles I., who was buried at Newton Valence. The ceiling of one of the sitting rooms represents the four Seasons, in foliage.

Mr. Rickman's House and Grounds are worth a visit. And the School, built principally by the liberality of the Butler family, promises much fruit.

GREATHAM,

on the borders of Woolmer ("Wolf-Mere") Forest, now under the direction of the "Enclosure Commissioner," is about to change the aspect it has worn from the days of William I.; when it appears to have had attractions for "Waleran, the Huntsman."

Its pretty little Church and School tell us what may be done to make "the wilderness blossom as the rose." A handsome monument records a close connection between the parish of Greatham and

HARTING,

in the Carylls, of Lady Holt. Dame Margery, daughter of Richard Freelond, of Greatham, was the pious Ancestress of a family that became conspicuous for their Jacobite attachments. A monument in the Chapel of the Scotch College in Paris, relates that " John Caryl, Baron de Dunford, Lord of Harting, Lady Holt, &c. forfeited all his property for James II. and III. " Uppark too, had its loyal representative, in Sir Edward Ford, in the time of Charles I.: but has since passed into the possession of the Fetherstonhaugh family. Once the Baronial seat of the Husseys, there was a House for lepers at Harting: while the same Husseys founded Durford Abbey: and thence arose the parish of

ROGATE.

W. H. Blaauw, Esq. has supplied full information on this head, in his history of " DUREFORD ABBEY. " The Churches of Rogate and Harting are of **Modern** style; although the latter had a Church in the days of Saxon rule. But still the neighbourhood has its liberal landed proprietors—as at Dangstein—now, to clothe, and educate for useful life, the destitute of the weaker sex; as in the days when Dame Pickering and Oliver Whitby lived at Harting. And Uppark still maintains its reputation for scenery all unrivalled, among the beauteous SOUTH DOWNS. For Nature knows but little of those changes which affect her Lords so frequently. But a change will touch the earth at last: and the *future* will have to relate, how much, or all of present interest has passed away.